Eustace Budgell

Memoirs of the lives and characters of the illustrious family of the Boyles; particularly, of the late eminently learned, Charles Earl of Orrery.

Edited by Donald Brady

Waterford Co. Council

Published by

Waterford Co. Council
Co. Library, Lismore,
Co. Waterford.

© 2003, Waterford Co. Council
Donald Brady

This edition is limited to 500 numbered copies

signed by the Editor

No..**47**

ISBN 0953202232

produced by Probe Marketing
probe@indigo.ie

Contents

For my parents Donald and Maura Brady without who's
enduring and unswerving support I would have achieved
very little.

Donald Brady

Acknowledgements

The production of a new edition of "*The family of the Boyles*" was suggested by the extreme rarity and fragility of the early editions only one copy of which is held by Waterford County Library. In addition the lack of footnotes and explanatory text makes much of it difficult for the modern reader to comprehend and appreciate.

The electronic version of the *Dictionary of National Biography*, *History of the Irish Parliament 1692-1800* by Edith Mary Johnston-Liik and several articles by Jack Lynch, particularly "*Preventing Play: Annotating the Battle of the Books*" were indispensable sources and have been extensively used.

The book's production would not have been possible without the wholehearted support of

> Anne Walsh, Evelyn Coady, Bernie Leahy, Eddie Byrne and other members of the County Library Staff
> The Monks of Mount Melleray (who kindly translated the Greek and Latin text)
> Julian C. Walton
> County Library Cavan
> Fidelma Connors, Probe Marketing

In conclusion, this work could not have been produced without the support of the members of Waterford County Council and the wholehearted commitment of Director of Services Peter Carey and County Manager, Donal Connolly.

Eustace Budgell, 1686-1737

Background

Eustace Budgell was born on 19th of August 1686. He was the son of Gilbert Budgell, D.D., of St. Thomas, Exeter, by his first wife Mary, only daughter of Bishop Gulston of Bristol. Her sister was the mother of Joseph Addison. He graduated on 31st of March 1705 at Trinity College, Oxford. He later entered the Inner Temple, and was called to the bar. He shared Addison's lodgings during the last years of the reign of Queen Anne. He began writing and had significant publications in the 'Spectator.' However, his early work is very akin to that of Addison, and it has been suggested that much of it may have been written by Addison himself. On the death of Budgell's father he inherited an estate worth £950 a year though it was encumbered with serious debt. Having being called to the bar, his cousin Joseph Addison encouraged him to take up alternative employment in Ireland.

Ireland

Addison had become secretary to Thomas Wharton, the new Lord-Lieutenant of Ireland. Wharton, the First Marquis of Wharton (1648-1715), had a reputation as one of the most unscrupulous men of his age. He came to Ireland in 1708 and continued in his post until 1710. He appointed Addison as his secretary and Addison in turn acquired the post of Under-Secretary for Budgell. Wharton's first action in the Irish Parliament of 1709 was to procure 'an admirable bill to prevent the growth of popery' by which it was enacted that the estates of the Irish papists should descend to their protestant heirs. Jonathan Swift who had a profound aversion to Wharton described him as 'an atheist grafted upon a dissenter,' and lampooned him describing him as being preoccupied with 'vice and politics, so that bawdy, prophaneness, and business fill up his whole conversation"

Budgell also acted as chief secretary to the Lords Justices, Deputy Clerk of the Council, and served as M.P. for Mullingar in the Irish Parliament. He takes credit for energetic and disinterested conduct during the strain put upon his office by the dispatch of troops to Scotland in 1715 Upon leaving Ireland in 1717 Addison procured for Budgell the place of accountant-general, worth £400 a year. He held this appointment from 10th August 1717 to 11th December 1718. Following the appointment of the Duke of Bolton in 1717 as Lord-Lieutenant, his secretary, Webster, quarrelled with Budgell, which led to Budgell's removal from office. From a pamphlet, which he published on returning to England, it seems that the dispute turned mainly upon a clerkship in the office that Budgell wished to keep for his brother, while Webster appointed a Mr. Maddockes. Following this dispute which Addison had endeavored to avert and the publication by Budgell of a pamphlet opposing the peerage bill, thus offending Sunderland, Addison's patron, the relationship between the two cousins shattered and was not renewed.

While in Ireland his duties included the administration of secret service money under the Chief Secretary. This task had previously been executed by Joshua Dawson who consequently deeply resented the appointment of Budgell. A letter from Addison dated 12th March 1715 written to Archbishop King illustrates the nefarious side of this business. He states that "I shall leave Mr. Budgell to lay before your Grace what has been usual as to the secret service money & take care to put it to the proper use. I am forced often to advance money here [in England] to take out warrants for gentlemen in Ireland, to pay messengers, & sometimes to relieve such indigent petitioners as are not able to carry on a just pretension, not to mention the article of stationary ware &c. and as I do not follow my predecessors in taking fees for recommendatory letters or any business done in England the usual allowances on this head will be an ease to me". This was acknowledged by King and payment dispatched by Budgell. During his period in office Budgell was nominated to 12 committees of the Irish Parliament.

Budgell served as M.P. for Mullingar for one Parliament, the first of George I, which was elected 1715, called 12th November 1715, and dissolved 11th June 1727 following the death of the King. The sessions were as follows:

- 12 Nov. 1715 – 20 June 1716
- 27 Aug. – 23 Dec. 1717
- 26 June – 2 Nov. 1719
- 12 Sept. 1721 – 18 Jan. 1722
- 29 Aug. 1723 – 10 Feb. 1724
- 7 Sept. 1725 – 8 Mar. 1726

He was not a popular member of parliament and created many enemies. This is illustrated by a letter of 28ᵗʰ January 1718, sent by the Speaker, William Conolly, to Charles Delafaye, Joint Chief Secretary 1715-7: "By all I can find here [Budgell] makes few friends and to my knowledge he has by his late conduct lost those that could have served him. He is in ye right to pray for Mr. Addison's life for when anything happens to him, Mr. Budgell (if I am not greatly mistaken) will fall as fast as he rose." Budgell then seeking a new post, Conolly concluded that it would be "a shamefull thing to heape more favours upon soe worthless a fellow".

During Budgell's time in Parliament the following interesting acts were passed

- *An Act to restrain Papists from being high or petty constables, and for the better regulating the parish watches.* (1715)
- *An Act for the better regulating the corporation of the city of Kilkenny, and strengthening the protestant interest therein, and punishing alderman Robert Connell, for withdrawing himself with the books and papers belonging to the said corporation.* (1717)
- *An act for amending an act, intituled, An act for the better and more effectual apprehending and transporting felons and others; and for continuing and amending several laws made in this kingdom for suppressing tories, robbers, and rapparees;: and also to prevent the listing of his Majesty's subjects to serve as soldiers in foreign service without his Majesty's licence.* (1721)
- An act to prevent marriages by degraded clergymen and popish priests, and for preventing marriages consummated from being avoided by precontracts, and for the more effectual punishing of bigamy. (1725)

South Sea Bubble

Following his departure from Ireland Budgell traveled around Europe. On his return to England he invested in the South Sea Company. This company was established in 1711 by Robert Harley, in the process of peace negotiations to end the War of the Spanish Succession. The company was given a monopoly of British trade with the islands of the South Seas and with South America. The monopoly was based on the expectation of securing extensive trading concessions from Spain in the peace treaty. These concessions barely materialised, however, so that the company had a very shaky commercial base. Nonetheless, it was active financially, and in 1720 it proposed that it should assume responsibility for the entire national debt, again offering its own stock in exchange for government bonds, a transaction on which it expected to make a considerable profit. The government accepted this proposal, and the result was an incredible wave of speculation, which drove the price of the company's stock from £128 in Jan., 1720, to £1,000 in August. Many dishonest and imprudent speculative ventures sprang up in imitation. In September 1720, the bubble burst. Banks failed when they could not collect loans on inflated stock, prices of stock fell, thousands were ruined (including many members of the government), and fraud in the South Sea Company was exposed. The bursting of the bubble, which coincided with the similar collapse of the Mississippi Scheme in France, ended the prevalent belief that prosperity could be achieved through unlimited expansion of credit.

Budgell lost £20,000 and wrote extensively on the affair. The Duke of Portland had lost a large estate in the same affair, and helped Budgell to circulate various pamphlets on the event. Portland, on being appointed governor of Jamaica, proposed to take Budgell as his secretary, but was informed "that he might take any man in England except Budgell".

Seeks entry to English Parliament

Budgell now fell into financial difficulties, which seem to have affected his mental stability. He is reputed to have spent £5,000 of his own money and afterwards £1,000 given to him by the Duchess of Marlborough, in attempts to get into the English Parliament.

He became involved in numerous lawsuits. Some of these concerned an estate in Essex, a moiety of which he had bought prior to his South Sea losses from a clergyman named William Piers, with whom he had intricate disputes. Budgell believed Piers to be in league with some powerful man, possibly Prime Minister Walpole, who sought to ruin him. He was arrested for debt, though in December 1732 he obtained a decree for £5 for illegal arrest by a bailiff, Budgell claiming that he was privileged as secretary to Lord Orrery. Budgell further declared that he was pursued by spies, and that various attempts had been made upon his life. In his writings of the period he indicated that he had considered suicide and it is clear that over time his mental stability rapidly degenerated.

Suicide

His grievances, particularly towards Walpole, are set out in various tracts. Budgell had become one of the Grub Street authors, and a contributor to the 'Craftsman.' In February 1733 Budgell started a weekly periodical, called 'The Bee,' which ran to nine volumes, and continued to June 1735. It is chiefly comprised of extracts from contemporary papers, but contains personal reflections and boasts of his connection with Addison. It also contains references to the affair that completed his ruin.

This involved a controversy over the will of Matthew Tindal, the deist, then over seventy, who had taken lodgings near Budgell. Tindal died on 16th August 1733, and his nephew, Nicholas Tindal expected to be his uncle's heir. A will was produced which gave £2,100, his manuscripts, and some property to Budgell, and appointed Nicholas his residuary legatee. It turned out that Tindal's whole property had effectively been disposed of and lent on bond to Budgell. One of the bonds for £1,000 had disappeared. Other suspicious circumstances came to light, and the nephew, after compelling Budgell to give up the few remaining assets, published a pamphlet. A public debate directed through pamphlets followed, with Budgell coming out worst.

On 4th May 1737, having been 'much disordered for two or three days,' and expecting an execution on his house, Budgell drove to Dorset stairs, filled his pockets with stones, took a boat, plunged overboard into the Thames, and was drowned. Some notes and money were found in his pockets, and he left a brief will leaving his meagre estate to his daughter, Anne Eustace, who was then aged 11. A rambling note was found on his desk. Subsequently the coroner's jury returned a verdict of lunacy.

Noted for his epigrams two of his most quoted are:

"Friendship is a strong and habitual inclination in two persons to promote good and happiness in one another"

"Don't believe your friends when they ask you to be honest with them. All they really want is to be maintained in the good opinion they have of themselves."

Introduction

It is difficult to think of a family that has had more influence in Ireland over several centuries than that of the Boyles. As a Northern nationalist and as a proponent of social justice, one can deeply resent the ruthless carnage that was inflicted on the Irish people during this period and one can also react with distaste to the privilege and social inequity of massive wealth. However, one must also recognize the positive factors and influences and we can particularly appreciate the value of the historical evidence that has been recorded over centuries through the archives of large estates. Evidence from the Irish side and specifically from the "lower orders" has been little recorded except in songs and poems. We can, by understanding the template applied by the "winning side" in its political, social and religious bias, decipher and elicit the real facts from the propaganda.

Richard Boyle was one of the most charismatic and influential figures in late 16th and early to mid 17th century Irish and British History. His adult and active life span covers a period of the most incredible turbulence, embracing the huge expansion of English maritime world power, the destruction of the Gaelic over lordship of Ireland, through the almost genocidal Elizabethan wars, through the subsequent and equally destructive Cromwellian tumults and settlement which he did not live to see concluded. His rise from relative obscurity to become the richest man in Ireland and England, his acquisition of vast tracts of land throughout Ireland by marriage, purchase and more nefarious means, his position at critical junctures in some of the most influential posts in the English Administration, his parenting of three of the most fascinating figures of the age (Roger Earl of Orrery, Robert scientist and formulator of Boyles Law, and Catherine Lady Ranelagh), the marriage of other members of the family into some of the most influential families in these Islands and finally the preservation of the estate in the family, be-it in the female line, to the present day, are all factors in one of the most incredible and enduring stories of the era.

Roger Boyle, 1st Earl of Orrery, played a pivotal role in the wars during the Confederation of Kilkenny, an even more central one in the

Cromwellian settlement and following the death of Cromwell he adroitly aided the restoration of the Stuart Dynasty. Not only was he noted as a soldier and statesman but subsequently gained fame as an author It is particularly important to note that the most decisive plantation settlements took place, not during the Elizabethan or Cromwellian periods, but during the two Stuart dynastic periods.

Richard Boyle 2nd Earl of Cork, inheritor of his father's title and largest estates, appears to be a less interesting but equally ruthless figure in the period. His role subsequent to the Restoration was largely concerned with the improvement of the family fortunes after the ravages of the wars.

Robert Boyle who was born in Lismore in 1627 is a central and defining figure in the development of modern science. During the organisation of a festival in 1991 to commemorate the tercentenary of his death, I realised he appeared to be little known or appreciated in his own country. The commissioning of a bust by John Coll, now located in the Lismore Library and unveiled by the President, Mary Robinson, on September 17th 1991 was used to highlight this deficit. Like many of his siblings, Robert was fostered, which despite his fathers claims to novelty, had for centuries been a practice amongst the Irish Chieftains. The first four years of Robert's life, spent in fosterage, became an area of particular personal interest and led to an exploration of the Lismore Papers for clues and accounts of this period. This research led to a conviction that the Lismore Papers formed a central and totally under explored reservoir for the political, economic and social history of 16th and 17th century Ireland.

The position of Catherine Boyle Ranelagh, as one of the most important female figures in Cromwellian and Restoration England, is another area of social history well worth research.

Charles Boyle, the 4th Earl of Orrery is a fascinating figure. His first career was as a soldier in the campaigns of Marlborough. He then became a government minister and proponent of scientific and astronomical research leading to the naming of a planetarium, "The Orrery" after him He was subsequently jailed for six months in the Tower of London on charges of complicity in the Jacobite plots. These charges were apparently a case of guilt by association, as some of his close associates were involved. Finally, his most notable claim to fame is his involvement in the *"Battle of the Books"* and the work of Swift. This debate was concerned with some of the most significant issues in late Renaissance literary and humanist philosophy and methodology. While *"The Family of the Boyles"* is both quirky and short, Budgell's work serves as an evocative if selective and biased introduction to the family. The publication of this edition is primarily intended as an appetiser and introduction to my work on the Lismore Papers and specifically the Papers of Richard Boyle on which I have spent some considerable time and research over the past five years and an edition of which I hope to publish in the next few years.

Donald Brady

Charles Boyle Earl of Orrery,
Baron Boyle of Marston in England,
& Baron Broghill in Ireland, and
One of the Knights of the Most
Antient Order of the Thistle.

MEMOIRS OF THE LIVES AND CHARACTERS OF THE ILLUSTRIOUS FAMILY OF THE BOYLES; PARTICULARLY, OF THE LATE EMINENTLY LEARNED, CHARLES EARL OF ORRERY,

in which is contained many curious pieces of English History, not extant in any other Author; Extracted from original papers and manuscripts, with a particular account of the famous controversy between the Honourable Mr. Boyle, and the Reverend Dr. Bentley, concerning the genuineness of Phalaris's Epistles; also the same translated from the original Greek,

By. E. Budgell, Esq.;

with an appendix, containing the character of the Honourable Robert Boyle, Esq.; founder of an Annual Lecture in defence of Christianity, by Bishop Burnet, and others. Likewise his Last Will and Testament. [The third edition, carefully corrected.]

To the honourable John, Earl of Orrery.

My Lord,

he following memoirs of your illustrious family, can be addressed to no man so properly as to your Lordship; yet though your Lordship may seem to have a most particular interest in them, I flatter myself they will neither be unacceptable or unuseful to the public. I am humbly of the opinion that there is no sort of writing of more real use and advantage, than a true account of the lives, actions, and characters of eminent men. At the same time it must be confessed, that there is no kind of writing, in which it is more difficult thoroughly to succeed. To say nothing of all the qualities requisite in a historian, who shall attempt to give the world the lives and characters of great men, there are, methinks, at least two things necessary to give his work the last degree of beauty and perfection. He ought, in the first place, to be master of all such particulars as can be learned from any papers or memoirs relating to the person whose life he writes, or from the testimony of those who were most intimately acquainted with him: but besides this, that he may be capable of giving the finishing strokes and nicest touches to the portrait he is drawing, it were highly to be wished that he himself should have been well, and personally acquainted, with the man whose life and character he pretends to deliver down to posterity. All who are judges in painting, know at first sight, a copy from an original; or in other words, a picture which is only taken from another picture, from a piece for which the original himself sat, and where the painter drew from the life. Whatever qualifications I may want as an historian, I am extremely happy in the two particulars last mentioned: I have, by your Lordship's favour, learned everything I could wish, relating to your illustrious father, either from written memoirs, or his familiar friends; and your Lordship is no stranger to the honour I had of being known to him, or to the kind opinion which, how little soever I might deserve it, he was pleased to conceive of me. I had not, indeed, the good fortune to be intimately acquainted with him, till about a twelvemonth before he died; but during that time, there was hardly a week passed, in which I had not the honour and advantage of his conversation several days, and for some hours alone. Your Lordship is not ignorant how much he loved a tête-à-tête. He seemed in this particular to have been of the same opinion with the late Mr. Addison,[1] who used frequently to say, that there was no such thing as real conversation between more than two persons.

It is true, that in all public companies your Lordship's father appeared a most accomplished and well-bred man; yet he seemed to reserve the greatest beauties of his mind for the conversation of those men whom he honoured with his friendship, when he talked to them single and alone. It was in such conversations, that with infinite pleasure and surprise; I have had opportunities of observing the vast and uncommon extent, both of his natural and acquired parts; of seeing how great a progress he had made in every branch of science, how perfect a master he was of several parts of learning, which in the opinion of most people, are hardly consistent with each other; how right a judgment he formed of things; and with how piercing an eye, and uncommon a penetration, he saw into the real designs and characters of men; how true a lover he was of his country; how sincerely he wished its prosperity; how much he detested slavery in all shapes, but more especially when he thought he saw it coming upon us, under the specious disguise of freedom and liberty.

Pardon me, my Lord, if I find myself melted into an uncommon degree of tenderness, at the remembrance of some particulars at those

---

1 **Addison, Joseph (1672-1719):** He was a poet essayist and critic who served as Under-Secretary in Ireland. In 1711 he launched the first issues of *The Spectator* and later married the Countess of Warwick.

times, when your noble father was pleased to call out the latent qualities of his mind, and to allow his soul to appear in all her beauties.

Suffer me, my Lord, under all my misfortunes, to reflect with some little satisfaction, perhaps, with a secret pride, that I have not been thought unworthy the friendship of an Halifax,[2] an Addison, and an Orrery.

There is one circumstance I thought never to forget: your Lordship's father was pleased to take me into the number of his friends, even at a time when I was unjustly pursued with the utmost cruelty by a man in great power;[3] and had laid such a scheme for my advantage, (without my knowledge,) as would, in all probability, have secured me from the rage of my implacable enemy.

The mean apprehensions and slavish behaviour of too many, who would have the world believe them great men, adds an higher lustre to such generosity, than anything I am able to say in its praise.

While I am capable to think at all, I must ever remember such favours with the utmost gratitude. At the same time, as an historian, there is a certain fidelity due to the public, which no consideration whatever should make a man break through. A character truly drawn, and without a blemish, is what, I fear, the world never yet saw. Horace is plainly of this opinion, when he says,

> *Vitiis nemo sine nascitur:*
> *Optimus ille est*
> *Qui minimis urgetur. –*

If I know your Lordship, you will forgive my writing with great freedom, and the utmost impartiality, while I am endeavouring to transmit to posterity, the characters of your great ancestors, nor expect that I should now stain a pen which was never yet prostituted to flattery.

---

2 **Montagu, Charles, Earl of Halifax (1661-1715):** The fourth son of George Montagu of Horton, he was educated at Westminster School and Trinity College Cambridge. He was an author, scholar wit and politician of note. Montagu was involved in various financial scandals and was a friend of Newton and Swift.

3 **Walpole, Robert (1676-1745):** He was the fifth of seventeen children and was twice married having seven children himself. Walpole became an M.P. in 1701, becoming "Prime Minister" later, a role he held for over 20 years. He was the first PM to live at Downing Street. Budgell, despite a lack of evidence considered Walpole as his great enemy

In the following sheets I have stolen some things, either from what I have heard you say, or from some short notes of your Lordship's which I have seen in writing; but I am pretty confident, that your Lordship will also pardon this plagiarism, since I thus frankly confess it, and since those just observations, which I have borrowed from you, are to the advantage of your beloved father.

Your Lordship's filial piety does indeed truly deserve the wonder and imitation of a degenerate age. The public has beheld your Lordship (under such circumstances, as, in the opinion of many, would at least have extenuated a different behaviour) less pleased with the acquisition of riches and honours, than afflicted with the loss of a father and a friend.

The great character he so justly acquired, places your Lordship in a very conspicuous point of light. Mankind will naturally fix their eyes upon your Lordship at your first entrance upon public business, and expect some uncommon instances of virtue from a son of the late Lord Orrery.

Your Lordship has already in some measure answered their expectations when on a late memorable occasion, you showed, with the united forces of reason and eloquence, how inconsistent a standing army is with the liberties of a free people.

Without a compliment, your Lordship seems fully qualified to do what your Country can reasonably expect from you. Those great natural parts which heaven has blessed you with, have been cultivated and improved by learning. There are, to my certain knowledge, many people who can produce such familiar letters of your Lordship's upon several subjects, as even your father himself need not have blushed to have wrote; And your Lordship was long since distinguished and remarkable for the most amiable virtues in private life; for an excellent husband, a tender father, and a firm friend.

I must not conclude, without entreating your Lordship's pardon for the liberty I have taken, to mention you in the manner I have done at the end of these memoirs. I could not well avoid it; the affair I there speak of having made some noise in the world, and being a passage in the life of the late Lord Orrery, which required and deserved to be fully explained.

That your Lordship may long enjoy your noble fortune, and that happiness you are blessed with in domestic life, and that the present Lord Boyle may find his own father the most worthy his imitation of all his ancestors, is the hearty wish of,

My Lord,
Your Lordship's
Most devoted,
And most obedient,
Humble servant,
[March 21 1732]
E. Budgell

Memoirs of the life and character of the Late Earl of Orrery, and of the family of the Boyles

harles, late Earl of Orrery, was descended from an ancient and a noble family, attended with a certain felicity, of which few families besides can boast; namely, that ever since it was first ennobled, there has been, at least, one of its descendants more remarkable and conspicuous for personal merit, and undoubted abilities, than for his Birth, Titles, or Estate. We are told, that the person, from whom this family is descended, was Sir Philip Boyle, a Knight of Aragon, who signalised himself at a tournament in the reign of Henry VI. But the first of the family who acquired a vast fortune, and was made a Peer, was Richard, (the youngest son of Roger Boyle, of Kent, Esq.) who is still so famous in Ireland, and so often mentioned by the Title of *The Great Earl of Cork.*

This extraordinary man was born in the City of Canterbury, October 3rd 1566. After having received his academical education in St. Bennet's College in Cambridge, and studied Law with great application for some small time in the Middle-Temple, finding his fortune vastly inferior to his spirit, and that he was unable to support himself like a gentleman in his own country, he resolved to travel.

I have before me some Memoirs written by this great man in the year 1632, at which time he was Lord Boyle, Baron of Youghal, Viscount of Dungarvan, Earl of Cork, Lord High-Treasurer of Ireland,

and one of the two Lords Justices for the Government of that Kingdom: He calls these his memoirs *True Remembrances*; and says, he left them behind him for the benefit and information of his posterity. They are written with an air of religion becoming a person who was in the sixty seventh year of his age, and with a certain noble plainness and simplicity truly worthy of a great man. Speaking of his arrival at Dublin, he gives the following account of it:

> "When I first arrived at Dublin, in Ireland, the 23rd of June 1588, all my wealth was then twenty seven pounds, three shillings, in money; and two tokens, which my mother had formerly given me, viz. a diamond ring, which I ever have since, and still do wear; and a bracelet of gold, worth about ten pounds; a taffety doublet cut, with and upon taffety; a pair of black-velvet breeches laced; a new Milan fustian suit laced, and cut upon taffety; two cloaks; competent linen and necessaries; with my rapier, and dagger."

This was a very small stock for a young gentleman to launch into the world upon: But the parts, address, and learning of Mr. Boyle soon made him remarkable in a country which was not, at that time, the most polite in Europe, and where an accomplished man was seldom seen. One of the two daughters[4] and coheirs of William Apsley, of Limerick, Esq; a young lady of great merit, and a fine understanding, fell in love with our adventurer; and, though her fortune was vastly superior to what Mr. Boyle could pretend to on the foot marriages are made in this age, yet her indulgent father, who was himself charmed with the young gentleman's conversation, suffered his daughter to marry him. His behaviour to this lady gave her no reason to repent of her choice: But she was soon taken from her beloved husband: She died in childbed of her first child, and the infant, a boy, was buried at the same time, and in the same grave with his mother.

Mr. Boyle was now a widower, and master of five hundred pounds per annum in land, besides money; all which he had acquired by his

---

[4] Apsley, Joan (d.14th December 1599): She was the first wife of Boyle and died in childbirth leaving him an estate worth £500 per annum

marriage. That Oeconomy which is the true mother of generosity, and for which this great man was so very remarkable, enabled him not only to live in a handsome manner, but to make some new purchases in the province of Munster. This drew upon him the envy of several great men, who began already to apprehend that his uncommon parts and abilities might, one day, make him their superior. Sir Henry Wallop,[5] at that time Treasurer in Ireland, Sir Richard Gardiner, Chief Justice of the King's Bench, Sir Robert Dillon,[6] Chief Justice of the Common Pleas, and Sir Richard Bingham,[7] Chief Commissioner of Conaught, laid their heads together how to ruin him: To effect this, each of them wrote to Queen Elizabeth, and complained, in their letters, that Mr. Boyle, who had come into Ireland but a few years since, a young man, without any fortune or estate, lived in such a manner at present, and made so many purchases, as evidently showed that he was supported by the purse of some foreign prince. They insinuated, that this prince was, in all probability, the King of Spain, who was known, at that time, to have thoughts of invading Ireland.

To give some colour to their pretended suspicions, they assured her Majesty, that Mr. Boyle had bought several castles and abbeys upon the sea coast, extremely fit to receive and entertain the Spaniards; and

---

[5] **Wallop, Sir Henry (1540?-1599)**: He served as Lord Justice of Ireland, and was the eldest son and heir of Sir Oliver Wallop of Farleigh-Wallop in the county of Southampton. Wallop was in 1579 offered the post of vice-treasurer to the Earl of Ormond in Ireland. He landed at Waterford on 12th Sept. The outbreak of the Desmond revolt altered his role and he became a major proponent of the Munster Plantation. He and Adam Loftus, Archbishop of Dublin, were appointed Lords Justices on 14th July 1582, posts in which they served until 1584. Subsequently he was appointed a commissioner for surveying the lands confiscated by the rebellion of the Earl of Desmond, and in April 1587 he was appointed a Commissioner for transfer of lands in the plantation. In May 1595 Wallop was granted the abbey, castle, and lands of Enniscorthy (formerly in the possession of Edmund Spenser), and later the Abbey and its lands of Adare. In 1596 he, and Sir Robert Gardiner held unsuccessful negotiations with Hugh O'Neill. He died on 14 April 1599 and was buried in St. Patrick's Cathedral.

[6] **Dillon, Sir Robert (d. 1597)**: He was eldest son of Thomas Dillon of Riverston. In 1569 he was made second justice of the newly formed presidency of Connaught. Dillon became Chancellor of the Irish exchequer on 5 June 1572 and Chief Justice in 1581 in succession to his great-uncle, Sir Robert Dillon. In 1591 he became one of the commissioners appointed to restore peace following O'Rourke's rebellion, and was later accused of corruption and cruelty in connection with the suppression of the rebellion. Following these accusations he was committed to prison, removed from the privy council, and in 1593 made to resign the Chief-Justiceship. In 1593 he was restored to his place in the council, perpetual obstacles were placed in the way of his trial and later the Lord-Chancellor declared him to be innocent of the charges brought against him. In 1594, Fenton wrote to Burghley that Dillon was to be restored to the Chief-Justiceship, and this decision was confirmed by patent of 15 March 1594-5. He retained this position until his death on 15 July 1597; after which he was buried in Tara church.

[7] **Bingham, Sir Richard (1528-1599)**: He was the governor of Connaught, and was the third son of Richard Bingham, of Melcombe-Bingham, Dorsetshire. He was trained as a soldier from youth, and had an expansive military career. In 1579 Bingham was sent to Ireland to aid in the suppression of the Desmond insurrection. In 1580 he was involved in the infamous Smerwick massacre. In 1584 he was appointed governor of Connaught. His period of administration was extremely brutal and included the massacre of a party of 3000 Scots, men women and children. In 1588 Bingham issued a decree that all Spanish sailors landing on the coast of his province should be brought to Galway and there executed. He afterwards claimed to have executed 1,000 of the enemy. In September 1598 Bingham returned to Ireland with five thousand men to assume the office of Marshal of Ireland, vacated by the death in battle at the Blackwater of Sir Henry Bagnall. Bingham died on 19th January 1599.

that he was strongly suspected to be a Roman Catholic in his heart.

Mr. Boyle had some intimation given him of these suggestions, which were equally false and malicious. He immediately resolved, with great prudence, not to stay till his enemies were empowered to try and judge him in Ireland, but to go himself into England, and convince the Queen, how unjustly he was accused. He was preparing to embark, when the General Rebellion broke out in Munster, and the rebels, seizing upon his estates, laid them waste in such a manner, *"as I could not say* (says he) *that I had one penny of certain revenue left me."* Having, through many dangers, and with great hazard of his life, got to Dingle, he procured a ship there to transport him to Bristol; from whence he went to London; and looking upon his fortune to be in a desperate condition, returned to his old chambers in the Temple, with an intent to renew his studies in the Law: However, when the Earl of Essex[8] was designed for the Government of Ireland, he made a shift to get himself recommended to his Lordship; and was received with the humanity, for which that great man was so remarkable, and which rendered him so justly popular.

Sir Henry Wallop, Treasurer of Ireland, and Mr. Boyle's great enemy, was sufficiently alarmed, upon hearing he was well with the Earl of Essex: The Great Knight, was not a little apprehensive, that this young gentleman, whose capacity he knew and feared, had been pretty inquisitive into his management of the public revenues in Ireland; and could tell some tales, that would do him no kindness. To prevent this, he renewed his former complaints against him to the Queen; and with so much success, that at last, by her Majesty's special direction, Mr. Boyle was taken up, and committed close prisoner to the gatehouse.

He had now nothing to support him, but his own courage and integrity: He was so conscious of the last, that he humbly petitioned the Queen he might be examined, and have leave to defend himself before her Majesty's Council; and that her Majesty would be graciously pleased to be present herself at his Examination and Defence.

---

[8] **Devereux, Robert, Earl of Essex (1566-1601):** He led an ill fated expedition to Ireland in 1599 and on his return to England he instigated plots against Queen Elizabeth leading to his imprisonment in the Tower and execution on 25th February 1601.

It is well known, that Queen Elizabeth loved to see with her own eyes, and hear with her own ears; and that she never refused an audience, even to the meanest of her subjects, who came to her with a complaint against any of her Ministers: To this conduct, so truly worthy a wife and good princess, and to that excellent judgement she showed in her choice of men of the greatest parts and capacities for her service, who were so many checks and spies upon one another; I say, to these two things, are evidently owing her prodigious successes, and all the glories of that reign, which makes the most shining part of the English history.

Her Majesty, though strongly prejudiced against Mr. Boyle, as conceiving that she had sufficient proofs of his guilt, yet readily consented to do him the justice to hear what he could say in his own defence. A day was therefore appointed for his appearing before the council, her Majesty being present.

Mr. Boyle having first fully answered whatever was alleged against him, gave a short relation of his own behaviour since he first settled in Ireland, and made it evidently appear, that he had acted like a good Englishman, and a loyal subject. He concluded, with giving her Majesty and the Council an account of the conduct of his chief enemy, Sir Henry Wallop, Treasurer of Ireland, and of that great knight's method in passing his accounts.

He had no sooner done speaking, than the Queen, who never countenanced oppression in the greatest of her ministers, who discovered an uncommon penetration, and was extremely happy in her judgement of men, broke out into the following words:

"By God's death, all there are but inventions against this young man, and all his sufferings are, for being able to do us service, and those complaints urged to forestall him therein; but we find him to be a man fit to be employed by ourselves, and will employ him in our service; Wallop, and his adherents, shall know, that it shall not be in the power of any of them to wrong him, neither shall Wallop be our Treasurer any longer."

To show she meant as she spoke, she ordered her Council to give her immediately the names of six men, out of which she might choose one to be Treasurer of Ireland. Her commands were instantly obeyed; and her Majesty having made choice of Sir George Carey,[9] rose from her seat, and publicly commanded, that Mr. Boyle should not only be discharged from his confinement, but be fully reimbursed for all the charges and fees his restraint had brought upon him. She then gave him her hand to kiss before the whole Assembly, and ordered him to attend the Court. This was looked upon as a certain indication, that she thought him a man qualified for her service, and resolved to employ him. People were not deceived: Her Majesty, a few days after, gave him the office of Clerk of the Council, of Munster; and commanded him to go over to Sir George Carey, the Lord President of that Province.[10]

Mr. Boyle, by the sole goodness and penetration of our renowned Queen, having thus triumphed over the malice of his enemies, bought a ship of Sir Walter Raleigh, called the Pilgrim, freighted her with ammunition and victuals, and arrived in her at Carrigfoyl-Kerry, before which, the Lord President and the Army then lay; and this castle being taken soon after, Mr. Boyle was there sworn Clerk of the Council of Munster, and made Justice of the Peace, and Quorum throughout all that Province: "*and this* (says the Earl of Cork, in his Memoirs) *was the second rise that God gave to my fortunes.*"

It is easy to imagine, that Mr. Boyle was received extremely well by Sir George Carey, the Lord President, since he was, at least, the remote cause of his Lordship's being made Treasurer of Ireland: He was with him at the Siege of Kinsale, and pitched upon by his

---

[9] **Carey, (or Carew) Sir George (d.1617):** He must be distinguished from Sir George Carew, Earl of Totnes and President of Munster. Carey was from Cockington, Devon, and was appointed Treasurer-at-war 1598-9 and a Lord Justice 24 Sept. 1599. On Mountjoy's departure in 1603 he became Lord Deputy of Ireland and died in February 1617.

[10] **Carew, (or Carey) George, Baron Carew of Clopton and Earl of (Totnes 1555-1629):** Carew was the son of George Carew, Dean of Windsor and was born on 29th May 1555. He was educated at Broadgates Hall (afterwards Pembroke College), Oxford. From an early age he devoted himself to military pursuits. In 1574 he entered the service of his first cousin, Sir Peter Carew in Ireland. He had a varied and extensive military career. Carew took part in Essex's expedition to Cadiz in May 1596, and in that to the Azores in 1597. On 27th January 1599-1600. Carew became president of Munster and lent Mountjoy major support in the suppression of the revolt. He was ruthless in his treatment of the Irish in Munster. Following the end of the rebellion he returned to England. Carew visited Ireland in 1610 to report on the condition of the country, with a view to a resettlement of Ulster, and described Ireland as improving rapidly and recovering from the disasters of the previous century. He was created Earl of Totnes on 5th February 1625-6 and died on 27th March 1629. Carew was a major bibliophile and took a great interest in Irish History. His papers inspired the detailed account of the Irish revolt (1599-1602), which was published in 1633, under the title of 'Pacata Hibernia, or the History of the late Wars in Ireland.' Much of his book collection found its way into the collections of the emerging major British Libraries.

Excellency to carry her Majesty the news of the great victory obtained over the Spaniards and Tyrone,[11] near that place:

> *"I made a speedy expedition to the Court,* (says the Earl in his Memoirs,) *for I left my Lord President at Shannon-Castle, near Cork, on the Monday morning about two of the clock, and the next day, being Tuesday, I delivered my packet, and supped with Sir Robert Cecil,*[12] *being then Principal Secretary, at his house in the Strand; who, after supper, held me in discourse 'till two of the clock in the morning; and by seven that morning, called upon me to attend him to the court, where he presented me to her Majesty in her bed-chamber."*

I transcribe this last passage from the Memoirs of that great man, of whom I am now speaking, with a good deal of pleasure; as it may serve to give my readers and idea of the virtue and manners of our ancestors, and to show into how shameful a degree of effeminate luxury we are since fallen. We see, in the passage last quoted, the Great Cecil calling upon a gentleman, when neither of them had slept five hours, and introducing him at seven in the morning to Queen Elizabeth in her bed-chamber. If we reflect upon the hours our Ministers keep at present, we shall be the less surprised to find, that our affairs are not managed altogether so successfully as in the days of Queen Elizabeth.

The expedition Mr. Boyle made to carry the news of this victory to the Queen was indeed so speedy, to use his own term, that I should have made some difficulty of believing the fact, if I had not seen it in his own Memoirs, which are evidently wrote without the least affectation, and with a great regard to truth.

---

[11] **O'Neill, Hugh, Earl of Tyrone (1540-1616):** The Great "Irish Rebel" he was the leader of the Irish cause in the 9 years war.

[12] **Cecil, Robert, Earl of Salisbury and first Viscount Cranborne (1563?-1612):** He was the son of William Cecil, Lord Burghley. In 1591 he was knighted and later that year joined the Privy-Council. He became Secretary of State in 1596. Cecil served in this capacity until the death of Elizabeth in 1603 and masterminded the transfer of power to King James. He continued as secretary under James I, and on 13 May was made Baron Cecil of Essendine, Rutland, on 20 Aug. 1604 Viscount Cranborne, on 4 May 1605 Earl of Salisbury, and on 20 May 1606 a knight of the Garter. He was lord-lieutenant of Hertfordshire from 1605 until his death.
Cecil served as Lord Treasurer from 6th May 1608 and from that time till his death the finances of the country came more than ever under his direction. He died on 24th May 1612.

"The Queen (continues the Earl) *remembered me, and calling me by my name, gave me her hand to kiss, telling me, that she was glad that I was the happy man to bring the first news of so glorious a victory; and, after her Majesty had interrogated with me upon sundry questions very punctually, and that therein I had given her full satisfaction in every particular, she gave me again her hand to kiss, and recommended my dispatch for Ireland, and so dismissed me with grace and favour."*

A man would be apt enough to think, upon reading the Earl's Memoirs, that his friend Sir George Carey, the Lord President of Munster, was Commander in Chief of the Queen's Forces when this victory was obtained; and it is observable, that the Earl always mentions this gentleman (to whom he had great obligations) with the utmost gratitude and respect: But the fact is, that when this happy victory was obtained, which obliged the Spaniards to leave Ireland and Tyrone, to fling himself at the Queen's feet, her Majesty's army was commanded in chief by the Lord Deputy Mountjoy[13] who succeeded Essex: The Lord Mountjoy was, indeed, assisted by the Lord President with that army which was under his command.

Mr. Boyle, upon his return to Ireland, found the Lord President ready to march with his army to the Siege of Berehaven Castle, which was at that time fortified, and possessed by the Spaniards and some Irish Rebels: His Excellency carried this place sword-in-hand, and gave no quarter to any of the garrison; after which he reduced the western parts of the Province; and having left proper garrisons in all places of importance, returned to Cork. In his way thither he told Mr. Boyle, that he resolved to send him into England, to obtain leave from Her Majesty, that he might himself repair to her royal Presence, and give her a full account of the posture of her affairs in Ireland. At the same time he advised him to buy all Sir Walter Raleigh's lands in Munster, and offered to befriend him in the purchase. Accordingly, when he dispatched him for England, he sent two letters by him;

---

[13] **Blount, Charles, Lord Mountjoy, 1st Earl of Devonshire (1563-1606):** He was sent as Viceroy to Ireland by Queen Elizabeth and was the victor of the long standing struggle with Hugh O'Neill and the other Irish Chieftains,. His victory paved the way for British domination in Ireland.

one of these was directed to Sir Robert Cecil, Secretary of State, in which he gave a very advantageous account of Mr. Boyle's great abilities, and of the services he had done his country; in consideration of which, he desired the secretary would introduce him to Sir Walter Raleigh, and recommend him to that great man, as a proper purchaser for all his lands in Ireland, if he was disposed to part with them. The Lord President's other letter was directed to Sir Walter himself, acquainting him, that the bearer, Mr. Boyle, was a person capable of purchasing all his estate in Ireland, which he presumed he would be glad to dispose of, since the management of it in those turbulent times gave him a great deal of trouble, and the income it produced was very inconsiderable. These letters occasioned a meeting between Sir Robert Cecil, Sir Walter Raleigh, and Mr. Boyle; at which the two last, by the mediation of the first, soon struck up a bargain, and proper conveyances were executed between them. These lands, though they had yielded but little to Sir Walter Raleigh, became soon after (when the war in Ireland was fully ended) a very noble estate to Mr. Boyle, who had purchased them. *"And this,* (says he in his Memoirs, when he was Earl of Cork,) *was a third addition and rise to my estate."*

About this time, upon his return to Ireland, in the year 1603, he began to think of taking a wife, that his posterity might enjoy the fortune providence had blessed him with. He made choice of Catherine, the only daughter of Sir Geoffrey Fenton,[14] principal Secretary of State in Ireland; and this was so entirely a match of inclination, that he desired no fortune with her.

> *"I never demanded* (says he in his Memoirs) *any marriage portion, neither had promise of any, it not being in my consideration; yet her father, after my marriage, gave me one thousand pounds in gold with her; but the gift of his daughter unto me, I must ever thankfully acknowledge, as the crown of all his blessings; for she was a most religious, virtuous, loving, and obedient wife unto me all the days of her life, and the*

---

[14] **Fenton, Sir Geoffrey, (1540-1608):** He came to Ireland as Surveyor-General and held various senior posts in the administration of Ireland. Fenton's daughter Catherine married Richard Boyle and he was buried in St Patrick's Cathedral Dublin in Archbishop Weston' tomb.

happy mother of all my hopeful children, who, with their posterity, I beseech God to bless."

On the 12th of March, 1606, he was sworn a Privy-Counsellor to King James I. by the Lord Chichester,[15] then Lord-Deputy of Ireland; and from this time, so great was the reputation of his wisdom and abilities, that few people cared to declare themselves his enemies; and his honours and estate constantly increased. In 1616 he was created Lord Boyle, Baron of Youghal. In 1620 he was created Lord Viscount of Dungarvan, and Earl of Cork; and on the 26th of October, 1629 he was sworn one of the Lord Justices for the Government of Ireland, in conjunction with the Lord Viscount Loftus, his Son-in-Law.

In the year 1631 he was made Lord High-Treasurer of Ireland. This honour was made hereditary to his family, and is, at this day, possessed by the present Earl of Burlington, his descendant, who is likewise Earl of Cork.

I have purposely omitted to mention the many important services performed by this great man to Queen Elizabeth, and her two successors, King James and King Charles I. These may be sufficiently collected out of the English and Irish history: My only design in these short memoirs, relating to him, was to mention some particulars not so generally known, and which might serve for openings to his character, should some abler pen undertake to write his life.

I cannot say in what year he died: He had no less than fifteen children, namely, seven sons, and eight daughters, by his beloved wife Catherine, daughter to Sir Geoffrey Fenton. I find that his last child, Margaret, was born in England, in the year 1629 at which time the Earl was in the 64th year of his age. He takes notice in his Memoirs of the birth of his daughter, in the following words:

---

[15] **Chichester, Arthur, Lord Chichester of Belfast (1563-1625):** He was Lord Deputy of Ireland, and was the second son of Sir John Chichester of Rawleigh, near Barnstaple. Following a successful military career he was appointed governor of Carrickfergus and the adjacent country by the Earl of Essex. Chichester played a small part in the Nine Years War. "Of any sympathy with the Irish character there is no trace in Chichester's letters. Like every Englishman of that day, he had no other recipe for Irish misery than the enforced adoption of English habits....'I wish,' he wrote on 14 March 1602, 'the rebels and their countries in all parts of Ireland like these, where they starve miserably, and eat dogs, mares, and garrons where they can get them. No course will cut the throat of the grand traitors, subject his limbs, and bring the country into quiet, but famine, which is well begun, and will daily increase. When they are down, it must be good laws, severe punishment, abolishing their ceremonies and customs in religion, and lordlike Irish government, keeping them without arms more than what shall be necessary for the defence of the honest, and some port-towns erected upon these northern harbours that must bridle them, and keep them in perpetual obedience"[DNB] He played a central role in the Plantation of Ulster. He died without issue and his brother Edward, father of Arthur Chichester, first earl of Donegal inherited.

"My fifteenth child, and eighth and last daughter, Margaret, was born in Channell-Row, in Westminster, April 30, 1629. The great God of Heaven I do humbly Beseech to bless all these my children, whom he hath in his mercy so gratefully bestowed on me, with long and religious lives; and that they may be fruitful in virtuous children, and good works, and continue till their lives end loyal and dutiful subjects to the King's Majesty and his Heirs, and approve themselves good patriots, and members to the commonwealth, which is the prayer and charge of me their father, in the 67th year of my age, 1632."

Of his sons, Richard, the second son, succeeded in the Earldom; Lewis was created Baron of Bandon, and Viscount Kinalmeaky; Roger was Baron of Broghill, and Earl of Orrery; and Francis was Lord Shannon; and though Robert, his seventh and youngest son, who survived him, never cared for a Peerage, which it is remarkable all his other brothers had, his personal merit gave him a value much above any title the Crown could bestow upon him, and has made his name famous, not only in England, but in every nation throughout Europe.

The Earl of Cork had the pleasure to see three of the five sons, who survived him, namely, Richard, Lewis,[16] and Roger, made Peers before his death; his son Francis was afterwards made Lord Shannon; and from these his sons, are descended the present Earl of Burlington, the Earl of Orrery, and Lord Shannon. We have already taken some notice of his youngest son Robert, and shall say more of him hereafter. The Lord Blessington,[17] in Ireland, whose name is also Boyle, is descended from the eldest brother of this our great Earl, for whom he procured the Bishopric of Cork.

Of his daughters, the Lady Alice was married to the Earl of Barrymore, Sarah to the Lord Digby, Lettice to the Lord Goring, Mary to the Earl of Warwick, Joan to the Earl of Kildare, Dorothy to the Lord Loftus, and Catherine to the Lord Ranelagh.

---

[16] Lewis did not survive him, dying at the Battle of Liscarroll in 1642.

[17] Boyle, Charles 2nd Viscount Blessington (1674-1732): He was the son of Murrough Boyle and Anne Coote. He had one son who died in infancy and subsequently his title passed to William Stewart.

I believe I may venture to affirm, that the founder of no family in England, was ever so far favoured by providence, as to see so many of his children settled in the world, and disposed of after so honourable a manner.

The Irish are still full of their praises of the Great Earl of Cork, whose Memoirs I am now writing, and tell a hundred stories of splendour in which he lived, of the exact order observed in his family, and of his generous behaviour to men of merit. He is allowed to have been a dutiful son, an excellent husband, a tender father, and a firm friend; and his estate, great as it was, seems plainly to have been acquired by honest methods, not by injustice, rapaciousness, and oppression. There are some traces of every particular I have mentioned in those short Memoirs, which he has left behind him. He speaks of his parents in the following handsome manner:

> *"My father, Roger Boyle Esq; was born in Herefordshire; my mother Joan Naylor, daughter to Robert Naylor, of Canterbury, in the County of Kent, Esq; was born there the fifteenth of October, in the twenty first year of King Henry VIII and my said father and mother were married in Canterbury the sixteenth of October, in the eighth year of Queen Elizabeth. My father died at Preston, near Feversham in Kent, the 24th of March, 1576. My mother never married again, but lived ten years a widow, and then departed this life, at Feversham aforesaid, the 20th of March, 1586 and they both are buried in one grave, in the upper end of the chancel of the Parish-Church of Preston; in memory of my deceased and worthy parents I, their second son, have, in 1629, erected a fair alabaster tomb over the place where they were buried, with an iron grate before it, for the better preservation thereof."*

He mentions the death of his lady, in the following tender words:

> *"My dear wife, the crown of all my happiness, and mother of all my children, Catherine Countess of Cork, was translated at Dublin from this life into a better the 16th of February, 1130,*

and was the 17th privately buried, in the night, in the upper end of the choir of St. Patrick's Church in Dublin, in the grave or vault wherein Dr. Weston, her grandfather, and good Lord Chancellor of Ireland, and Sir Geoffrey Fenton, his Majesty's Principal Secretary of State for this realm, her father, were entombed: Her funerals were honourably solemnized in public the 11th day of March, Anno Dom. 1629. In the perpetual memory of which my virtuous and religious deceased wife, and of her predecessors and posterity, I have caused a fair tomb to be erected, with a cave or cellar of hewed stone underneath it. I have purchased from the Dean and Chapter of St. Patrick's Church the inheritance of that upper part of the chancel, wherein the cave or cellar under ground is made, and whereon the tomb is built, to be a burying-place for me, my posterities, and their children."

He took the utmost care of the education of his children; and had the satisfaction to see that it was not flung away upon them.

His eldest son Roger died when he was nine years old, and lies buried at Deptford in Kent. His second son Richard succeeded to the Earldom; and he mentions this son in his Memoirs after the following manner:

"My second son Richard was born at the College of Youghal the 20th of October, 1612. The Earl of Thomond,[18] Sir Richard Aldworth,[19] and Mr. Thomas Ball of London, were his Godfathers, and Lady Anne Parsons Godmother. God grant he may serve and fear him religiously, and be a faithful subject and servant to the King's Majesty and his heirs, and live many years full of good works, and of virtuous children, and be a worthy pillar and patriot in this kingdom. He being Viscount of Dungarvan, was knighted in my house at Youghal the 13th

---

[18] **O'Brien, Donough (d.1624):** The date of his birth is uncertain, but he succeeded as 4th Earl of Thomond in 1581.

[19] **Aldworth, Sir Richard (d.1629):** On December 6th 1615, Sir Richard Aldworth received a grant of land consisting of the areas Aghatrasney and parts of Carrigcashel and He was Provost-Marshal in Munster until his death on 21st June 1629. He is buried in Christ Church cemetery, Newmarket.

of August, 1624, by the Lord Falkland,[20] *Deputy-General of Ireland: And my said son departed Dublin, to begin his travels into foreign kingdoms the 4th of June, 1632, I allowing him one thousand pounds a year in his travels."*

He mentions Sir George Carey, Lord President of Munster, with the utmost gratitude, declaring, that his Lordship dealt with him not only nobly, but like a father; and having once had a sort of a friendship with Sir Henry Wallop, he vows to God, that he never should have done that gentleman any prejudice, if he had not been forced to it by the base and cruel usage we have already given an account of.

Lastly, speaking of his settling in Ireland, and of the estate he had acquired there, he has the following words:

"The blessing of God, whose heavenly providence guided me hither, hath enriched my weak estate in the beginning with such a fortune as I need not envy of any of my neighbours, and added no care nor burden of my conscience thereunto."

I am afraid, that few men who have acquired large fortunes of late years, can say what the Earl does in those remarkable words which close this last paragraph: His relying upon the Divine Providence, and gratitude for favours he had received from it, are prettily expressed by that humble motto, which he placed under his Arms, viz. *God's Providence is my Inheritance.* It is certain that providence accompanied his large fortune, which he assures us has honestly acquired, with great and unusual blessings. My readers cannot but have observed, how infinitely happy he was in his children; and though the virtues of great men are not often seen to devolve upon

---

[0] **Cary, Sir Henry, First Viscount Falkland (d.1633):** He was the son of Sir Edward Cary, Knight, of Berkhamstead and Aldenham, Hertfordshire. He studied at Oxford and subsequently served in France and the Low Countries. Later Cary became comptroller of the household and a privy councillor, and on 10th November 1620 Viscount Falkland. He was elected M.P. for Hertfordshire 11th December 1620. Chiefly through the favour of Buckingham he was appointed to succeed Viscount Grandison as Lord Deputy of Ireland, being sworn 18th September 1622. He proved bigoted and ineffectual. To raise funds for the government Cary convened an assembly of the nobility of Ireland on 22nd September 1626, before which he laid a draft of concessions promised by Charles, which were subsequently known as the 'Graces.' These promised the removal of certain religious disabilities and the recognition of sixty years' possession as a bar to all claims of the crown based on irregularities of title. He had significant differences with the Lord Chancellor Lord Loftus particularly in his attempt to achieve a plantation in Wicklow, that led to his removal in August 1629. Sustaining a broken leg, he died in September 1633.

their posterity, there are some of the descendants of this Earl still living, who seem to have degenerated from their illustrious ancestors.

Richard Boyle, common called the Great Earl of Cork, was succeeded in his Earldom by Richard, the eldest of his five sons, who survived him. I know little more of this nobleman, than what we learn from public history, namely, that he was remarkably eminent for his loyalty to King Charles I whom he assisted and supplied with money in his troubles; that he married Elizabeth, sole daughter and heir to the Earl of Cumberland; was at first created Lord Clifford of Lanesborough; and afterwards, in farther consideration of his faithful services to the Crown, both in England and Ireland, was created Earl of Burlington. He had two sons by Elizabeth his wife: his youngest son Richard was killed at sea in the war with the Dutch in which he behaved with great gallantry. His eldest son Charles, commonly called Lord Clifford, died also before him; so that he was succeeded in his honours and estate by his grandson, the issue of his eldest son Charles, by a daughter of William Duke of Somerset.

This Charles, who succeeded his grandfather, was generally looked upon to be one of the best-bred men in England. He was gentleman of the bed-chamber, and one of the Privy-Council to King William. In the first year of the reign of Queen Anne, he was made Lord Lieutenant of the West-Riding in Yorkshire, and appointed one of her Majesty's commissioners to treat of an Union with Scotland; But dying the same year, he was succeeded in his honours and estate by his son Richard, who is at present both Earl of Burlington and Earl of Cork.

I shall be more particular in my account of Roger, the third son of the Great Earl of Cork, who survived his father; who made so considerable a figure in the Camp, the Court, and the Republic of Letters; who was first created Baron of Broghill, afterwards Earl of Orrery, and was grandfather to the late Earl of Orrery; to whose memory these memoirs are chiefly dedicated.

Roger Lord Broghill, and the first Earl of Orrery, was born on the 26th of April 1621. At the age of fifteen, he was sent to the College of Dublin; where after he had followed his studies for some time, and acquired the reputation of being a good scholar, he was ordered by his

135, 643

father to set out for his travels under the care of one Mr. Marcombes,[21] who was made his Governor. The first court he went to, was that of France, where he saw Louis XIV in his nurse's arms; and from thence went into Italy. Upon his return from his travels, going to the English Court, he appeared to be so accomplished a young man, that both the late Earl of Northumberland, and the Earl of Strafford endeavoured to gain him. By the first, he was entrusted with the command of his own troop in his expedition into the North of England against the Scotch: By the latter, he was encouraged to hope for any honour or employment that lay in his power to procure for him; and was actually created Baron Broghill, by the mediation of this great favourite.[22]

He was married soon after to the Lady Margaret Howard, sister to the Earl of Suffolk.

I have just perused a manuscript, which, I am informed, was never yet printed, entitled, *Memoirs of the most remarkable passages in the life and death of the Right Honourable Roger Earl of Orrery*, written by Mr. Thomas Morrice, his Lordship's Chaplain. The Earl had a particular kindness for this gentleman, and would talk to him with great freedom. Mr. Morrice, by these memoirs, appears to have been a very religious and honest, but a very weak man: He has larded his work with several silly stories about witchcraft, Calvin, and Dr. Deodato; yet, as he had great opportunities of knowing some things, and seems a man of too much honesty and integrity to aim at imposing upon the world, I should think myself inexcusable, if I did not borrow some particulars from him: I shall, however, make use of his manuscripts with great caution, and endeavour to avoid those errors in several historical facts, which he has most evidently, though I dare say, not willingly committed. The valuable part of his manuscript is those particulars which he either saw himself, or learned from his patron's own mouth.

Lord Broghill, soon after his marriage, took his lady with him into Ireland, where they arrived the very day on which the great rebellion

---

[21] **Marcombes, Isaac (1608-1665):** Tutor and companion to the four Boyle children on their continental tours.

[22] The intervention by Strafford as suggested by Budgell is incorrect. As Grossart has stated Roger Boyle was created Baron Broghill at least six years before the intervention by Strafford mentioned. Considering the relationship between him and the Boyle family it would have been very unusual for Strafford to make such a proposal.

broke out. It was not, however, then known in Munster, that the Irish had taken arms; so that he landed without opposition, and conducted his lady to Lismore, a mansion-house of his father's.

A day or two after his arrival, he waited on his father at Castlelyons, where the Earl of Barrymore, his brother-in-law, had invited them both to dine. The Lord Muskerry, and some other men of quality of the Irish Nation, with whom they lived in an easy and familiar way, were of the party. Just before dinner a messenger arrived, who could not be persuaded to sit down, till he had spoke in private with the Earl of Cork, whom (with horror in his face) he acquainted, that the Irish were in open rebellion, and had committed the most un-heard-of cruelties on those unhappy English who fell into their hands; that the rebels were masters of all the country he had passed through; and that he had brought his Lordship this Intelligence with the utmost hazard of his life.

The Earl without showing any marks of surprise, returned to his company, and dined with them; but as soon as dinner was over, acquainted them with the news he had received.

My Lord Muskerry, who was a facetious man, and an excellent companion, employed all the wit he was master of to turn the whole story into ridicule; and took upon him to assure the company that their Intelligence must be false. They were, however, so much alarmed, that they immediately repaired to their respective houses, where the next news they heard was, that the Lord Muskerry appeared at the head of some thousands of Irish.

Under this terrible calamity the Earl of Cork summoned in his English tenants, and made up a body of five hundred men, in which little army Lord Broghill had the command of a troop of horse.

The rebellion now becoming universal, and being attended with that bloody massacre, of which our histories give a particular account, the Lord Broghill and his brothers were ordered to join the Lord President St. Leger[23] with the troops under their command; which they

---

[23] **St. Leger, Sir William (d. 1642)** He was the son of Sir Warham St. Leger and was probably born in Ireland, but the date is uncertain. He went to Holland, and served in the army for at least eight years. St. Leger was knighted on 25 April 1618, and in 1619 he had a large grant of lands in Ireland. On his return to Ireland in July 1627 he was made Lord President of Munster and a privy councillor. On the outbreak of the rebellion in 1641 St. Leger had few resources to defend his province. He was ruthless but his activities were those of containment until his death in 1642.

did accordingly, though with little success, the number of the rebels being so much superior to that of the English.

The Lord Broghill, however, had frequent opportunities of showing that he wanted neither conduct nor courage.

Upon the first breaking out of the Great Irish Rebellion, an Act passed, to which his Majesty gave the Royal Assent, and by which the reducing of Ireland was entirely committed to the management and care of the Parliament, who issued out commissions to several persons to go over into Ireland, and subdue the Rebels. The Marquis of Ormond, at last, by the King's express command, surrendered the Government of Ireland, and the City of Dublin, to the Parliament Commissioners; and the Lord Broghill, with several others, zealous Royalists, acted under them for some time against the rebels: But now the King's affairs became desperate in England, and his Majesty underwent that hard fate that every body knows.

The Lord Broghill was so shocked at the news of the King's death, that he immediately quitted the service of the Parliament; and looking upon Ireland, and the estate he had there, as utterly lost, he embarked for England, and retired to Marston, a seat which he had in Somersetshire, where he lived privately till the year 1649.

In his retirement he could not, however, forbear reflecting upon the miserable condition both of his country and the Royal Family, till at last he conceived it beneath his spirit and quality, to see the public ruined, and his own private fortune enjoyed by rebels. He resolved therefore to attempt something, both for the sake of his country and himself; and accordingly under the pretence of going to the Spa for his health, he determined to cross the seas, and apply himself to King Charles II for a commission to raise what forces he could in Ireland, in order to restore his Majesty, and to recover his own estate. Having taken this resolution, he applied himself to the Earl of Warwick, who had an interest in the prevailing party, desiring him to procure a licence for him to go to the Spa. He pretended to the Earl, that he meant nothing more by this journey, than the recovery of his health; but let some of his friends of the Royal party, in whom he thought he could confide, into the bottom of his design; and having raised a considerable sum of money, came up to London, to prosecute his voyage.

I have heard a certain great man, who knew the world perfectly well, often assert, that, a secret was never kept by three persons. His Lordship had entrusted his secret to more than three; and the Committee of State, who spared for no money to get proper intelligence, being soon made acquainted with his whole design, determined to proceed against him with the utmost severity. Cromwell was at that time General of the Parliament-Forces, and a member of the Committee. It is allowed by his enemies, that this wonderful man knew every person of great abilities in the three Kingdoms: He was consequently no stranger to Lord Broghill's merit; and reflecting, that this young nobleman might be of great use to him in reducing Ireland, he earnestly entreated the Committee, that he might have leave to talk with him, and endeavour to gain him, before they proceeded to extremities. Having with great difficulty obtained this permission, he immediately dispatched a gentleman to the Lord Broghill, who let him know that the General, his master, intended to wait upon him, if he knew at what hour he would be at leisure.

The Lord Broghill was infinitely surprised at this message, having never had the least acquaintance, or exchanged a single word with Cromwell. He therefore told the gentleman, that he presumed he was mistaken; and that he was not the person to whom the General had sent him. The gentleman readily replied, that he was sent to the Lord Broghill; and therefore if he was that Lord, that he was sent to him. His Lordship finding there was no mistake in the delivery of the message, confessed that he was the Lord Broghill: He desired the gentleman to present his humble duty to the General, and to let him know, that he would not give him the trouble to come to him, but that he himself would wait upon his Excellency, if he knew at what hour it would be most proper for him to do so; and that in the mean time, he would stay at home, to receive his further commands. The gentleman replied, that he would return directly, and acquaint his General with what his Lordship said.

The Lord Broghill in the meantime was under a good deal of concern, at what should be the meaning of this message. He never once suspected that his design was discovered; but while he was musing in his chamber upon what had passed, and expected the return of the gentleman, he saw Cromwell himself, to his great surprise, enter the room. When some mutual civilities had passed between them, and they were left alone, Cromwell told him in few words, that the Committee of State were apprised of his design of going over, and applying to Charles Stuart for a commission to raise forces in Ireland; and that they were determined to make an example of him, if he himself had not diverted them from that resolution. The Lord Broghill interrupted him here, and assured him, that the intelligence the Committee had received was false; that he was neither in a capacity, nor had any inclination to raise disturbances in Ireland; and concluded with entreating his Excellency, to have a kinder opinion of him. Cromwell, instead of making any reply, drew some papers out of his pocket, which were the copies of several letters the Lord Broghill had sent to those persons in whom he most confided, and put them into his hands. The Lord Broghill, upon the perusal of these papers, finding it was to no purpose to dissemble any longer, asked his Excellency's pardon for what he had said, returned him his humble thanks for his protection against the Committee, and entreated his directions how he ought to behave in so delicate a conjuncture. Cromwell told him, that though till this time he had been a stranger to his person, he was not so to his merit and character; that he had heard how gallantly his Lordship had already behaved in the Irish Wars; and therefore since he was named Lord Lieutenant of Ireland, and the reducing that kingdom was now become his province, he had obtained Leave of the Committee to offer his Lordship the Command of a General Officer, if he would serve in that war; that he should have no oaths or engagements imposed upon him, nor be obliged to draw his sword against any but the Irish Rebels.

The Lord Broghill was infinitely surprised at so generous and unexpected an offer: He saw himself at liberty by all the Rules of Honour, to serve against the Irish, whose rebellion and barbarities were equally detested by the Royal Party and the Parliament. He desired, however, the General to give him some time to consider of what had been proposed to him. Cromwell briskly told him, that he must come to some resolution that very instant; that he himself was returning to the Committee, who were still sitting; and if his Lordship rejected their offer, had determined to send him immediately to the Tower. The Lord Broghill finding that his liberty and life were in the utmost danger, and charmed with the frankness of generosity of Cromwell's behaviour, gave him his word and honour, that he would faithfully serve him against the Irish rebels. Upon which Cromwell once more assured him, that the conditions he had made with him, should be punctually observed; and then ordered him to repair immediately to Bristol, to which place forces should be sent to him, with a sufficient number of ships to transport them into Ireland. He added, that he himself would soon follow him; and was as good as his word in every particular.

The Lord Broghill, pursuant to the Lord Lieutenant's Order, hastened to Bristol, where everything was soon sent to enable him to pass over into Ireland. Upon his arrival in that kingdom, so much had he gained the affections of all who had served him before, that they immediately repaired to him; so that he had soon a troop of horse, which consisted all of gentlemen, and a Regiment of fifteen hundred men well appointed. With these he hovered up and down the country, till the Lord Lieutenant himself landed with an army of twelve thousand horse and foot, whom he joined at Wexford.

The Lord Broghill had been advised by some of his friends to have a care of Cromwell, not to put himself in his power, but to act at least at the head of a separate army. His Lordship considering how much encouragement it would give the rebels, should they perceive any jealousies among those who acted against them, resolved entirely to rely upon the Lord Lieutenant's honour, nor found any reason to repent of his confidence.

Everybody has heard of Cromwell's successes in Ireland: He began with attacking Drogheda; and omitting to make his approaches in a regular manner, and according to the forms of war, took a town by storm, garrisoned with three thousand men, which had held out three whole years against all the fury of the Irish rebels. Echard[24] says, that

---

[24]**Echard, Laurence (1670?-1730):** He was a historian and Religious Minister. He was the son of the Rev. Thomas Echard of Barsham, near Beccles, Suffolk. Echard studied at Cambridge, where he graduated with a B.A. in 1691 and M.A. in 1695. Echard, having been ordained became chaplain to the Bishop of Lincoln. For more than twenty years he resided in Lincolnshire and during that time published many works including in 1707 his 'History of England" which was amended in 1718 by a further two volumes and finally in 1720 by an appendix. He also published 'An Exact Description of Ireland,' &c., 1691". He died at Lincoln, while on his way to Scarborough on 16th August 1730, and was buried in the chancel of St. Mary Magdalen's Church.

when the famous rebel O'Neill heard of this action, he swore that if Cromwell had taken Drogheda by storm, if he should storm hell, he would take that too. His following successes were equal to this beginning: impatient to end the war, that he might return to England, he pushed on his conquests, even in the depth of winter. The Lord Broghill did his duty so well upon all occasions, that Cromwell was highly satisfied with his behaviour in general, but more particularly with the gallant action he performed during the siege of Clonmel.

The Lord Lieutenant having determined to besiege this place, had intelligence brought him, that all the country was in arms before him; that they had already formed a body of troops, which was daily increasing, and had resolved to relieve Clonmel: he therefore ordered the Lord Broghill, with a strong party, to fall upon those Irish which were got together, while he himself sat down before Clonmel. The Lord Broghill, in obedience to the Lord Lieutenant's commands marched at the head of his party into the west; where he fell so briskly and unexpectedly upon the body of the enemy, consisting of between four and five thousand men, that he entirely defeated them.

He had no sooner obtained this victory than he received a letter from Cromwell, acquainting him with the miserable condition his army was in before Clonmel: he let him know that most of his men were sick of the bloody-flux, the disease of the country; that they had already been twice repulsed by the Irish; and that he should be obliged to raise the siege, if he was not immediately joined by his Lordship: he therefore conjured him, by all the ties of duty and friendship, to think no longer of dispersing the rebels in the west, but to come immediately to him.

The Lord Broghill, when he received this letter, was taking proper measures to prevent the enemy, whom he had defeated, from forming themselves again into a body; but upon receiving so positive a command from Cromwell, he immediately sent him word, by his own messenger, that by the blessing of God he had just defeated the enemy, and would not fail to be with him in three days, Cromwell was infinitely pleased upon the receipt of this message; and when the Lord Broghill, at the time he had promised appeared at the head of his party, Cromwell made the whole army before Clonmel, cry out,

A Broghill! A Broghill! At the same time, he ran to him, and embracing him in his arms, highly applauded his courage and conduct, and gave him joy of his late victory. The Lord Lieutenant being thus reinforced, took Clonmel in the depth of winter.

Soon after this, Cromwell was sent for by the Parliament to oppose the Scotch: upon which, making Ireton[25] his deputy, and Commander in Chief of the forces in Ireland, and leaving Lord Broghill at the head of a flying-camp in Munster, he embarked for England. Lord Broghill with his little army, took several places, routed the enemy in several encounters, and gave undeniable proofs of great conduct, and an undaunted courage, hazarding his own person upon several occasions with the utmost frankness and gallantry. His successes and victories, joined to the affability of his behaviour, acquired him so great a reputation, that Ireton (who suspected he had still an hankering towards the Royal Party) is reported to have said to one or two of his friends, we must take off Broghill, or he will ruin us all.

Mr. Morrice, in his memoirs, says positively, that his patron received a letter from one Lieutenant, who was Ireton's Chaplain, but a great friend of the Lord Broghill's, wherein he advised him to take care of himself, because Ireton, not withstanding all his professions of friendship, and kind letters to congratulate him upon his successes, had privately determined to destroy him, that upon this information, the Lord Broghill kept at a distance from Ireton as long as he had any pretence for doing so, but that being commanded to join him, in order to form a siege of Limerick, he was obliged to obey.

During the siege of this place, he performed a very gallant action: he was commanded by Ireton to prevent the Lord Muskerry's joining the Pope's Nuncio, who had already got together a body of eight

---

25 **Ireton, Henry (1611-1651):** He was he the eldest son of German Ireton of Attenborough, near Nottingham. He was a major military figure on the Parliamentary side in the English Civil War. Ireton accompanied Cromwell to Ireland as second in command. Following a significant campaign he took Ardfinnan Castle on the Suir. On 4th January 1650 the parliament appointed him president of Munster. Ireton's regarded the replantation of the country with English colonists as the only means of permanently securing its dependence on England. "He ordered the inhabitants of Limerick and Waterford to leave those towns with their families and goods within a period of from three to six months, on the ground that their obstinate adherence to the rebellion and the principles of their religion rendered it impossible to trust them to remain in places of such strength and importance". (DNB) After the capture of Limerick Ireton caught fever, and died on 26 Nov. 1651. Parliament ordered a state funeral and his body was conveyed to London, and interred on 6th February 1652 in Westminster Abbey. On the Restoration the House of Commons ordered the bodies of Cromwell, Ireton, Bradshaw, and Pride "to be exhumed, drawn to Tyburn, there to be hanged up in their coffins and after that buried under the gallows". This sentence was carried into effect on 26-30 January 1661

thousand men, and determined, as soon as he was joined by Muskerry, to attempt the relief of Limerick. The Lord Broghill had but six hundred foot and four hundred horse assigned to him for this service. He marched with so much expedition, that he came up with Muskerry before he was able to join the Nuncio: Muskerry was at the head of one thousand horse and dragoons, and about two thousand foot; notwithstanding which the Lord Broghill fell resolutely upon him. The charge was desperate on both sides: the Irish who were three to one, at last surrounded the English, but offered the Lord Broghill fair quarter; who to encourage his men, exposed his own person wherever the enemies seemed most likely to prevail. His Lordship refusing to accept of the quarter which was offered him, the Irish cried out, kill the fellow in the gold-laced coat; which in all probability they had done, if a Reformado Lieutenant,[26] of his own troop, had not come in to his rescue; who, before he could bring him off, was shot twice himself, and had his horse killed under him. The English, after the example of their Commander, resolving now either to conqueror or die, fought with so desperate a courage, that they at last routed their enemies, of whom they killed six hundred upon the spot, and took a good number of prisoners.

If Ireton intended to destroy the Lord Broghill, which is a very doubtful point, his death prevented the execution of his design. He took Limerick; but died a few days afterwards of the plague in that city. Cromwell, who survived him, seemed determined to attach the Lord Broghill to his service by none but the most generous methods, namely by loading him with fresh favours. The wars of Ireland being finished, he sent for him over into England, where he was now declared Protector, made him one of his Privy Council, and (though perhaps he trusted no man more than he was obliged to) seems to have allowed him as great a share of his confidence as to any man except Thurloe:[27] nor do I think there can be a greater instance of Cromwell's

---

[26] **Reformado Lieutenant**: An archaic term referring to an officer left without a command (due to the 'reforming' or disbanding of his company) but retaining his rank and seniority, and receiving full or half pay; A volunteer serving in the army without a commission, but with the rank of an officer.

[27] **Thurloe, John (1616-1668):** He was Secretary of State to Cromwell; M.P. for Ely, 1656, and for the University of Cambridge in Richard Cromwell's Parliament of 1658. He was never employed after the Restoration, although the King sought his services.

fine taste, and how much in his heart he despised that cant he was often obliged to use, than the visible pleasure he took in the conversation of the Lord Broghill, Mr. Waller, and Milton.

About this time, Cromwell wanting a dexterous man to preside in Scotland, cast his eyes upon the Lord Broghill. His Lordship, who was sensible that great but ticklish post might prove his ruin, would have declined accepting it; but Cromwell telling him that it was necessary for his service, Broghill was obliged to submit: however before he went into Scotland, he obtained a promise of the Protector, that he would be recalled in one year, and that his Highness would believe no complaints that might be made against him, till he had an opportunity of vindicating himself. Cromwell, conformable to this promise, recalled him at the end of one year; and though, as Lord Broghill had foreseen, the most violent complaints had been made against him, Cromwell would credit none of them, till he had heard what his Lordship could say for himself. Upon his return to London, he gave so clear an account of his conduct in every particular, and of the reasons which induced him to act as he had done, that Cromwell conceived a much higher esteem for him than ever.

He made use of his interest with the Protector to do a great many generous things; and Cromwell, who knew how well he loved to be employed in a good-natured action told him one day in a gay manner, that an old friend of his was just come to town. The Lord Broghill desiring to know whom his Highness meant? Cromwell to his great surprise, answered. The Marquis of Ormond. Lord Broghill protesting he was wholly ignorant of it. *I know that well enough* (says the Protector;) *however, if you have a mind to preserve your old acquaintance, let him know, that I am not ignorant either where he is; or what he is doing.* He then told him the place where the Marquis lodged; and Lord Broghill having received this generous permission to save his friend, went directly to him, and acquainted him with what had passed, who finding himself discovered, instantly left London, and with the first opportunity returned to the King.

Soon after, Cromwell being informed, that the Lady Ormond was engaged in several practices against his Government, and corresponded with her husband, for the better accomplishing of them, he resolved to use her with great severity and told the Lord Broghill with a frown, the first time he saw him, *You have passed your word for the quiet behaviour of a fine person; The Lady Ormond is in a conspiracy with her husband against me, though, at your request, I permit her to stay in London, and allow her 2000 per annum. I find she is an ungrateful woman, and shall use her accordingly.* Lord Broghill who saw the protector was thoroughly provoked, but knew that a soft answer usually appeased him, told him in the most submissive manner, that he was sorry the Lady Ormond had given his Highness any occasion to be displeased with her, but humbly desired to know, what ground he had for suspecting her? *Enough:* (says Cromwell,) *I have letters under her own hand, which were taken out of her cabinet:* And then throwing him a letter, bid him read it. He had no sooner perused it, than he assured the Protector with a smile, that what he had read was not the hand of Lady Ormond, but of Lady Isabella Thynne,[28] between whom and the Marquis of Ormond, there had been some intrigues. Cromwell hastily asked him, how he could prove that? Lord Broghill answered, very easily; and showed him some other letters from the Lady Isabella; of whom he told two or three stories, so pleasant, as made Cromwell lose all his resentment in a hearty laugh.

Being a member of Cromwell's Parliament, he gave so handsome a character in the House of Commons of the Lord Clanricarde,[29] a Roman Catholic, though he had no personal acquaintance with him, that it prevented those severe revolutions which the House had otherwise come to against that unfortunate nobleman.

I ought not to omit acquainting my readers, that Mr. Morrice, in his manuscript, says, that the Lord Broghill kept up a constant correspondence with King Charles the Second during his exile. It is

---

[28] **Thynne Isabella**: She was the daughter of Henry Rich 1st Earl of Holland who was beheaded by Parliamentary forces during the Civil War. She was the Granddaughter of Sir Walter Cope who in 1602 had erected Castle Cope, subsequently renamed Holland House in Kensington. She married James Thynne and is said to have seen a 'fectch' a double or co-walker, a death portent as her sister had done just prior to her death.

[29] **Burgh, Ulick de 5th Earl of Clanricarde (1604-1657)**: He was born at London in 1604, was the only son of Richard, fourth earl of Clanricarde. He sat in the parliament of 1639-40, and accompanied Charles I in his expedition to Scotland. Clanricarde was made governor of the town and county of Galway, and, as owner of vast estates in that district, he exercised great influence there. During the revolt in 1641 he supported the Royalist side but managed to be included among the persons 'excepted from pardon for life and estate,' under the 'Act for the settling of Ireland,' passed in 1652. Clanricarde died at his English residence in Kent and was buried at Tunbridge.

not impossible, that after the restoration his Lordship might be well enough pleased to have this believed; might suffer his honest chaplain to think for himself, and to report it to others; but if I am not much mistaken, his Lordship's whole behaviour, and that generosity of temper which is so remarkable in him, plainly contradict this story. I take the truth of the matter to have been thus: He was by principle inclined to the Royal Party, but overcome at last by the many favours conferred upon him by Cromwell, (who seldom failed of gaining those he condescended to court,) he zealously attached himself to the interest and service of the Protector. What confirms me in this opinion, is, that my Lord Clarendon[30] speaks of the Lord Broghill just before the King's restoration in the following manner:

"The Lord Broghill, who was president of Munster, and of a very great interest and influence upon that whole province, though he had great wariness in discovering his inclinations, as he had great guilt to refrain them, yet hated Lambert[31] so much, that he less feared the King; and so wished for a safe opportunity to do his Majesty service; and he had a good post, and a good party to concur with him, when he should call upon them, and think fit to declare." It is scarce to be conceived, but that if the Lord Broghill had kept a constant correspondence with the King in his exile, my Lord Clarendon must have known something of it: Besides, though I have no mean opinion of the Lord Broghill's dexterity, I do by no means think him a match for Cromwell; or that the Protector was capable of being thus imposed upon. It appears very plain to me, that after the death of his Patron Cromwell, he did his best to have served his son; but when Richard was set aside, the Lord Broghill was no longer obliged by any particular ties of gratitude, to serve those who assumed the Government; and finding most of their schemes wild and ill-concerted,

---

30 **Hyde, Edward, first Earl of Clarendon (1609-1674)**: He was descended from a family of Hydes who were established at Norbury in Cheshire.

31 **Lambert, John (1619-1684):** He was born near Skipton, Yorkshire. On the outbreak of the first Civil War, Lambert joined the Yorkshire Parliamentarians and quickly rose to the rank of colonel. He played an active role in the Civil War and was later promoted to Major-General. He was appointed second-in-command to Cromwell against Charles II and the Covenanters. He refused to take the oath of loyalty when Cromwell was installed as Lord Protector for life and resigned his commissions, retiring to his residence in Wimbledon. Prior to the restoration Lambert was imprisoned in the Tower by Parliamentary forces and while he escaped, he was recaptured and jailed. He spent the rest of his life in prison and following the death of his wife in 1676 he became insane and died in February 1684.

he might probably think, that nothing was so much for the good of his country, as to restore the Royal Family; for from this period of time, it is very certain, that no man in the three Kingdoms was more active or zealous in contriving a method for his Majesty's return.

Richard Cromwell, upon the death of his father, chose the Lord Broghill, Dr. Wilkins,[32] and Colonel Philips, to be his Cabinet-Council. His Lordship was likewise a member of that Parliament which was called by the new Protector.

Richard was prevailed upon at the same time the Parliament met, to consent to the meeting of a General Council of Officers, and did this without consulting his own Cabinet Council. The Lord Broghill no sooner heard of it, than he went to the new Protector, and desired to know if his Highness had really consented to the meeting of a General Council of Officers: Richard told him he had. *I fear* (says Lord Broghill) *your Highness will soon repent it; and that they will certainly work some mischief against yourself and your friends.* Richard told him, that he hoped he would do what he could to prevent it. To which Broghill replied, that as a General Officer, he had an undoubted right to assist at the Council, and would most certainly be there, to observe what they aimed at. Then turning to the Lord Howard,[33] and Lord Falconbridge, who happened to be present, he told them, he hoped they would both assist, and stand by him. They faithfully promised they would. On the day when the General Council was to meet, the three Lords went altogether to Wallingford-House. They found above five hundred officers assembled. After a long prayer made by Dr. Owen,[34] Major-General Desborough[35] rose up, and in a

---

[32] **Wilkins, John (1614-1672):** He was Bishop of Chester and a strong supporter of the Parliamentary Cause but managed to hold his position after the Restoration.

[33] **Howard, Charles 3rd Earl of Nottingham (1610-1681):** He was born on 25th December 610 at Haling House and died on 26th April 1681

[34] **Owen, Dr John (1616-1683):** A theologian he was born of Puritan parents at Stadham in Oxfordshire in 1616. At twelve years of age he was admitted at Queen's College, Oxford, where he took his B.A. degree in 1632 and M.A. in 1635. He supported the Parliamentary cause and subsequently became pastor of Coggeshall in Essex. While there he founded a church on Congregational principles. He met and Cromwell and was brought to Ireland with him as chaplain and also to regulate the affairs of Trinity College. In March 1660, the Presbyterian party being uppermost, Owen lost his deanery. He retired to Stadham, where he spent most of the rest of his life in the production of religious pamphlets. He died at Ealing, on August 24th 1683, and was buried in Bunhill Fields.

[35] **Desborough, John (1608-1680):** He was the second son of James Desborough of Eltisley, Cambridgeshire. He became a renowned Parliamentary Major-General in the English Civil war. Desborough married Jane, sister of Oliver Cromwell, on 23rd June 1636. He opposed the succession of Richard Cromwell and supported more radical elements in Parliament. On the restoration he was briefly held in custody but due to insufficient evidence was allowed to retire into relative obscurity.

long speech put them in mind, how gracious the Lord had been, and how their arms had prospered; though he feared this prosperity would not last long, since several sons of Belial[36] were crept in amongst them, who in all probability would draw down the judgements of Heaven upon them. To prevent this, he thought it would be convenient to purge the army; and that the best method of doing so, would be to propose a test, which all persons who refused to take, should be turned out; that the test he proposed was, that every one should swear, that he did believe in his conscience, that the putting to death of the late King Charles Stuart, was lawful and just.

This proposal of Desborough's was received with great applause by most of the Assembly, who cried out well-moved! And the Lords Howard and Falconbridge thinking it in vain to oppose so apparent a majority, rose up and went to the Protector, to let him know what was doing. Lord Broghill, who had his wits about him, though vexed to see himself deserted by his two friends, as soon as the Assembly was silent, rose up in his place, and declared, that he was not of the same opinion with the noble Lord who spoke last; that he was against imposing any test upon the army, as a thing they had often declared against; and that if they once came to put tests upon themselves, they would soon have them put upon them by other people, and consequently lose that liberty of conscience, for which they had so often fought; that he was against the particular test proposed, because he thought it unjust and unreasonable to require men to swear to the lawfulness of an action, which they were not present at; that many gentlemen, on whom he had his eye, besides himself, were not present when the late King was put to death; and therefore could not swear to the lawfulness of a proceeding, the circumstances of which they were unacquainted with; but that if they would have to test to purge the army, he conceived he had as good a right to propose one as another man, and therefore should take the liberty to offer one, which he hoped would be found more reasonable and more lawful than that mentioned

---

36 **Belial** is found frequently as a personal name in English translations of the Bible, and is commonly used as a synonym of Satan or the personification of evil. Milton, however, distinguishes Belial from Satan regarding him as the demon of impurity. In the Hebrew Bible, nevertheless, the word is not a proper name, but a common noun usually signifying "wickedness" or "extreme wickedness". Thus, Moore renders "sons of Belial" as "vile scoundrels" less fellows"

by the noble Lord who spoke before him: He then proposed, that all persons should be turned out of the army who would not swear to defend the established Government under the Protector and Parliament. This test, he said, was reasonable, since their own being depended upon it; and lawful, because it was to maintain the present Government. He added, that if this test should have the ill fortune to be rejected in that Council, he would move it the next day in the House of Commons, where he was pretty confident it would meet with a better reception.

Upon the conclusion of this mettled speech, there was a louder cry of Well-moved! than when Desborough had spoke before. While the noise continued, and the Assembly was in some confusion, Lord Broghill changing his place, and getting between Colonel Whalley[37] and Gough,[38] two hot men, and easily fired, used such arguments to them, that each of them in a warm speech declared for the test last proposed. Fleetwood[39] and Desborough, with some of their most trusty friends, finding it impossible now to carry that test, which would have modelled the army as they desired, retired to consult what was to be done. After a short stay, they returned to the Council, and declared, that they had seriously considered of what the Lord Broghill had said: They confessed, that they had not at first seen all the ill consequences of imposing tests upon the army, but they were at present fully

---

[37] **Whalley, Edward (d. 1675?):** He was second son of Richard Whalley of Kirkton and Screveton, Nottinghamshire. He joined the Parliamentary forces on the outbreak of the Civil War and rose rapidly to the rank of Lieutenant-Colonel. On the formation of the new model in 1645 Cromwell's regiment was divided into two parts, and command of one of them was given to Whalley. He was appointed on 6th January 1649 as one of the commissioners for the trial of the king and signed the death-warrant. As a regicide he was excluded from the act of indemnity. Following the Restoration the government offered a reward for his arrest. But before this was issued Whalley, with his son-in-law, Major-general William Goffe fled to Boston and he died in America circa 1675.

[38] **Goffe or Gough, William (d.1679?):** He was the son of Stephen Goffe, rector of Stanmer in Sussex. In 1642 was imprisoned by the royalist Lord Mayor of London for promoting a petition in support of the parliament's claim to the militia. He joined the model army and served with distinction He was named as one of the king's judges and signed the death-warrant. Before the Restoration he succeeded in escaping, and was excepted from the Act of Indemnity, and a proclamation was issued on 22nd September 1660 for his arrest (In company with his father-in-law, Lieutenant-general Whalley, Goffe landed at Boston in July 1660. They moved to Newhaven, which they reached 7 March 1661. In October 1664 they removed to Hadley in Massachusetts, Goffe seems to have died in 1679. He was buried with Whalley, who had predeceased him, at Hadley.

[39] **Fleetwood, Charles (d.1692):** He was the third son of Sir Miles Fleetwood of Aldwinkle, Northamptonshire. A supporter of the parliament cause in 1649 he became Governor of the Isle of Wight. Fleetwood's importance was further increased by his appointment as Commander-in-chief in Ireland and his marriage to Cromwell's daughter Bridget widow of Henry Ireton. He remained in Ireland from 1652 until 1655, becoming Lord Deputy in 1654, until superseded by Henry Cromwell in 1657. The chief work of Fleetwood's government was the transplantation of the Irish landholders to Connaught. Following the death of Cromwell Fleetwood played a non-descript part in the succession and after the restoration his escape from prosecution was due to the fact that he had taken no part in the king's trial, and was not regarded as politically dangerous. Following the death of second wife Bridget he married again and resided at Stoke Newington. He died on 4th October 1692.

convinced of them: To avoid which, and that they might remain united amongst themselves, they proposed, that both the tests which had been offered, should be withdrawn; to which the Lord Broghill, after some little stiffness, consented. The method he took to ward off this first blow, which was aimed at the power of his master, the new Protector, was extremely dexterous: He knew very well, that if Fleetwood and his friends had spoke against the test he proposed, they would have rendered themselves odious, not only to Cromwell and the Parliament, but to many of their own party, who were not yet sensible at what they were aiming.

The Council broke up about eight of the clock at night, and adjourned till the next day. Upon the rising of the Council Lord Broghill went directly to Richard the Protector, whom he found with the Lords, Howard and Falconbridge. Having gently reproached these two noblemen for having deserted him in the day of battle, he was answered, that finding it impossible to oppose the torrent, and that Fleetwood and Desborough were sure of carrying their point, they thought themselves obliged to come away, and inform the Protector of what was doing. The Lord Broghill then, to their no small surprise and satisfaction, gave an account of his success; but added, that he plainly saw this Council would do mischief, if they were suffered to sit any longer. He therefore humbly advised the Protector, to dissolve them immediately. Richard asked, in what manner he should do it? Lord Broghill answered, that if his Highness pleased, he would draw up a short speech for him, which he might deliver at the General Council the next morning, after having sat amongst them about an hour. Richard promised he would do so. Upon which Broghill immediately drew up a short speech. The next day, at ten in the morning, the Protector, as had been agreed, went to the Council, and to the surprise of the Assembly, seated himself in a Chair of State, which had been placed there for him. After having listened to their debates about an hour, he rose up, and, with a much better grace than was expected from him, delivered himself to this effect:

"Gentlemen,
I thankfully accept of your services. I have considered your grievances; and think the properst method to redress what is amiss

amongst you, is to do it in the Parliament now fitting, and where
I will take care that you shall have justice done you. I therefore
declare my commission for holding this Assembly to be void; and
that this general Council is now dissolved; and I desire that such
of you as are not Members of Parliament, will repair forthwith to
your respective commands."

Had Richard continued to act with the same resolution and dignity he expressed upon this occasion, he might, in all probability, have held that power which was devolved upon him by the death of his father.

The speech above mentioned, though extremely mild, was a thunder-clap in the ears of Fleetwood, Desborough, and all their party: They immediately guessed the Lord Broghill was the author of it, and resolved to fall upon him in Parliament. Accordingly, when the house met, they complained, (with their eyes fixed on Lord Broghill,) that they had been highly abused and affronted by a certain Noble Lord in that Assembly; that they thought themselves obliged to demand satisfaction; and therefore humbly moved, that an Address should be presented to his Highness the Protector, to know, who had advised him to dissolve the Council of War, without the consent or knowledge of his Parliament. Some of the Lord Broghill's friends, who saw the storm was pointed at him, made signs to him to withdraw. His Lordship, however, sat still till his enemies had done scolding, when he rose up, and spoke in the following manner:

"Mr. Speaker,
I am not against presenting this Address; but humbly move,
that another may be presented to the Protector at the same time,
to know who advised the calling of a General Council of
Officers without the consent or knowledge of the Parliament;
for surely, if that man is guilty who advised the dissolution of
this Council, those people are much more guilty, who durst
advise his Highness to call such a Council, without either the
knowledge or consent of his Parliament."

The house, who suspected the Council of War was no friend to their power, was highly pleased with this second motion: They cried out,

Well-moved! and Fleetwood had the mortification to see himself baffled a second time by the dexterity of the Lord Broghill.

Though the Protector had dissolved the Council of Officers, a great number of them continued to meet privately, and resolved to omit no methods to oblige him to act as they would have him. The Lords Howard, Broghill, and some other officers, being informed of these meetings, told Richard plainly, that they thought not only his power, but even his person was in danger: that the behaviour of Fleetwood and his party, made it absolutely necessary for him to strike a bold stroke. They advised him therefore to remember, that he was Cromwell's son, and to act as his father would have done on such an occasion. They, lastly, offered, that if he would not be wanting to himself, and give them a sufficient authority to act under him, they would either force his enemies to obey him, or cut them off. Richard startled at this proposition answered, in a consternation, he thanked them for their friendship; but that he neither had done, or would do any person any harm; and that rather than a drop of blood should be spilt on his account, he would lay down that greatness, which was but a burden to him. He was so fixed in this resolution, that whatever the Lords could say, was not capable of making him alter it; and they found it to no purpose to endeavour to keep a man in power, who would do nothing for himself. The Council of Officers, soon after, this, sent some of their members to him; who, partly by threats, and partly by promises, obliged him to issue a proclamation for the dissolution of the Parliament; and as the Parliament were the only body of men capable to have supported him against the cabals of Fleetwood and his party, when the Protector signed the Proclamation for dissolving them, he, in effect, divested himself of all authority.

The Lord Broghill finding the family of Cromwell laid aside, to whom he had the highest obligations, resolved from this time, to do his utmost to restore the King; and for the purpose, to repair forthwith to his command in Munster, where he had a considerable power, and was greatly beloved. He arrived happily in Ireland, having escaped the ambushes which Fleetwood and Desborough had laid for him; who, fearing his enterprising genius, endeavoured to have apprehended him.

Soon after his arrival in Munster, the Committee of Safety, which was set up by the army, sent seven commissioners to take care of the affairs in Ireland. These commissioners had their instructions, to have a particular eye on the Lord Broghill, and, if possible, to take some occasion to confine him.

In the meantime, the Lord Broghill was setting all his wits at work to bring back the King. He truly judged, that the ill-concerted schemes of those who had usurped the supreme power in England, could not last long; and finding himself at the head of a considerable force in Munster, he determined to get the whole army in Ireland to join with him in his design; to gain Sir Charles Coote,[40] if possible, who had a great power in the north; and then to send to Monck[41] in Scotland.

While he was busied in these thoughts, a summons came to him from the Parliament Commissioners lately arrived, which required him to appear forthwith before them at the Castle in Dublin. He acquainted his most intimate friends with this message; who all advised him to stand upon his guard, and not put himself in the power of his enemies: But as he thought himself not strong enough yet to take such a step, he resolved to obey the Commissioners Summons. Taking therefore his own Troop with him as a Guard, he set out for Dublin. When he came to the City, leaving his Troop in the suburbs, he acquainted the Commissioners, that in obedience to their commands, he was come to know their farther pleasure. The day after his arrival, the Commissioners met in Council; and the Lord Broghill appearing before them, they told him, that the State was jealous he would practice against their Government; and that therefore they had orders to confine him, unless he would give sufficient security for his peaceable behaviour. He desired to know what security they expected. They told him, that since he had a great interest in Munster, they only desired him to engage, on the forfeiture of his life and estate, that there should be no commotion in that Province. He now plainly saw

---

[40] **Coote, Charles, First Earl of Mountrath, (1610-1661):** A major military figure in the Cromwellian wars, he was particularly noted for his savagery. His title passed to his son and became extinct on the death of the 7th Earl in 1802.

[41] Monck, George (Duke of Albemarle) (1608-1676: A professional soldier, he switched sides from the Royalist to Parliamentary forces early in the Civil War. He proved an able and successful General. He had little difficulty in supporting the Restoration.

the snare that was laid for him; and that if he entered into such an engagement, his enemies themselves might raise some commotion in Munster. He saw himself, however, in their power; and mad no manner of doubt, but that if he refused to give them the security they demanded, they would immediately clap him up in a prison. He therefore desired some time to consider of their proposal; but was told, they could give him no time, and expected his immediate answer. Finding himself thus closely pressed, he humbly desired to be satisfied in one point, namely, if they intended to put the whole power of Munster into his hands? If they did, he said, he was ready to enter into the engagement they demanded; but if they did not, he must appeal to all the world how cruel and unreasonable it was, to expect he should answer for the behaviour of those people over whom he had no command.

The Commissioners found themselves so much embarrassed with this question, that they ordered him to withdraw; and as soon as he had left the Council-Chamber, fell into a warm debate amongst themselves, and were of very different opinions how they ought to proceed with him.

At last Steele,[42] who was not only one of the Commissioners, but also Lord Chancellor of Ireland, declared,

> *"He was afraid, that even the honest party in Ireland would think it very hard to see a man clapped up in prison, who had done such signal services to the Protestants; but that on the other hand, he could never consent to an increase of the Lord Broghill's power, which the State was apprehensive might one day be employed against them."*

He therefore proposed, that things should stand as they did at present; that his Lordship should be called in, sent back to his command in Munster in a good humour, and be suffered, at least, to

---

[42] **Steele, William, (d.1680):** He was born in Cheshire, was an avid supporter of the Parliamentary cause, and was appointed one of Four Counsels in the trial of Charles I. He was subsequently nominated as one of the Council for the Government of Ireland and on 26th August 1656 was created Lord Chancellor. On the death of Cromwell Steele took part in the proclamation of Richard Cromwell in Ireland. But on Cromwell's removal in 1659 he was nominated as one of the five commissioners to govern Ireland. Later that year he returned to England and on the restoration he fled to Holland but returned to England prior to his death.

continue there till they received further instructions from England.

This proposal was agreed to by the majority of the Board; and Lord Broghill, being called in, was told, in the most obliging manner, that the Board was so sensible of the gallant actions he had performed in the Irish Wars, and had so high an opinion of his honour, that they would depend upon that alone for his peaceable behaviour. He was invited the same day to dine with the Commissioners; who omitted no caresses which they imagined would sweeten him before he left Dublin. The Lord Broghill, though he disguised his real sentiments under a frank and open air, looked upon their civilities in the manner they deserved; and upon his return to Munster, applied himself as closely as ever, to form a party for the King's restoration. After he had made sure of his own Officers, the first person of weight he engaged in the design, was the Governor of Limerick, in which place there was a garrison of two thousand men; and having now secured all Munster, he sent a trusty agent to Sir Charles Coote, to persuade that gentleman to do in the North of Ireland, what he himself had done in the South. Sir Charles readily came into the design; and having in a short time taken proper measures in the North, the Lord Broghill's messenger returned to him with an account of his happy success; and his Lordship being now empowered by most of the Chief Officers in Ireland, under their hands, dispatched his brother, the Lord Shannon, with a letter to the King, then in Flanders, acquainting his Majesty with the measures he had taken, inviting him to come into his Kingdom of Ireland, and assuring him, that if he pleased to land at Cork, he should be received by such a force, as was sufficient to protect him against all his enemies. At the same time, he dispatched a messenger to General Monck, then on his march from Scotland, to let him know what they were doing in Ireland, and to persuade him to do the like.

His Majesty was infinitely pleased at the receipt of Lord Broghill's letters; but received letters from England soon after, to acquaint him, that in all probability, he would be very soon invited thither.

The Lord Shannon was scarce embarked for Flanders, when his brother, the Lord Broghill, received a letter from Sir Charles Coote, to acquaint him, that their design of declaring for the King, or what was the same thing, for a Free Parliament, had taken air; and that he had therefore been obliged to declare somewhat sooner than the time they had agreed upon, and conjuring his Lordship, to declare himself likewise, and not to leave him in a design which he had first persuaded him to embark in.

The Lord Broghill, though he was a little apprehensive that the early step Sir Charles had taken might ruin their design, resolved not to desert his friend; and immediately declared himself. By this means those who had taken upon them the Government of Ireland, finding themselves in the midst of two powerful parties, made little or no resistance; and the Lord Broghill and Sir Charles Coote secured that Kingdom for his Majesty.

Upon the King's restoration, the Lord Broghill went into England, to congratulate his Majesty upon his happy return; but to his great surprise, instead of being thanked for his services in Ireland, was received with the utmost coldness. At last, with the assistance of his brother, the Lord Shannon, he discovered that Sir Charles Coote had not only sent over Sir Arthur Forbes[43] to the King, while he was at Brussels, to give his Majesty a favourable opinion of him, but to make his merit the greater, had himself assured his Majesty, since his restoration, that he was the first man that stirred for him in Ireland; that the Lord Broghill opposed his Majesty's return; and was not at last brought to consent to it without much difficulty.

The Lord Broghill, upon this information, no longer wondered at the cold reception he had met with. He recollected, however, that he had Sir Charles Coote's letters still by him, which we have just mentioned, and in which there were these words:

---

[43] **Forbes, Sir Arthur, first Earl of Granard (1623-1696):** He was the, eldest son of Sir Arthur Forbes of Corse in Aberdeenshire, who went to Ireland in 1620 with the Master of Forbes's regiment and was granted large estates in Leitrim and Longford by James I. His father was killed in a duel in 1632, and he was raised by his mother. During the rebellion of 1641 his mother was besieged in Castle Forbes for nine months, and Forbes raised men for her relief. He fought in Scotland on the King's side and following the defeat of Montrose in 1645 he was taken prisoner, and for two years confined in Edinburgh Castle. In 1660 Forbes was sent to Charles II to support his restoration. After the Restoration he received additional grants of land in Westmeath and in 1661 he entered parliament as member for the family borough of Mullingar. In 1675 he was created Baron Clanehugh and Viscount Granard. In 1684 Forbes became the Earl of Granard. He opposed James and supported William and was placed by the latter in command of a force of five thousand men for the reduction of Sligo, the surrender of which he secured. Forbes's last years were spent at Castle Forbes, where he died in 1696.

"Remember, My Lord, that you first put me upon this design; and I beseech you forsake me not in that which you first put me upon, which was to declare for King and Parliament."

The Lord Broghill put this letter into the hands of his brother Shannon, and conjured him to take care that his Majesty might see it. The Lord Shannon did so; and his Majesty, now fully convinced how serviceable the Lord Broghill had been to him, looked upon his Lordship with as gracious an eye, as he could himself desire or expect.

After this we are not to wonder that his Lordship was soon created Earl of Orrery, taken into his Majesty's Cabinet-Council, made one of the Lords Justices for the Government of Ireland, and Lord President of the Province of Munster.

Upon the King's restoration, the people of England seemed, for some time, to be in a continual jubilee. Adversity had given their young monarch such accomplishments, as princes seldom learn in any other school. His affability and good nature so agreeably dazzled the eyes of his subjects, that it was a long time before they either could, or would see any faults in him. His court was all splendour and gaiety; he was himself master of a good deal of wit, and consequently had a quick relish for works of genius. There was no foreign war; and the Earl of Orrery (so we must call Lord Broghill for the future) finding there was no longer any occasion for his sword, resolved to employ his wit and learning for the diversion and amusement of his Royal Master.

With this view he wrote his plays; which were most of them received upon the stage with the highest applause; and so much countenanced by the Court, that in the first play, called Henry V, Mr. Harris,[44] who acted the king, was dressed in the Duke of York's coronation suit; Mr. Betterton,[45] who played Owen Tudor, in King Charles's; and Liliston,

---

[44] **Harris, Joseph (?) (d.1681):** He was an actor known as "Mr. Harris" and due to confusion with a lesser actor, Joseph Harris (1661-1699) led to the ascription to him of the name Joseph. Harris's first recorded part was Alphonso in D'Avenant's 'Siege of Rhodes,' in which he appeared in 1661. He became one of the most celebrated actors of his era and was one of the three actors to whom, on the production of 'Love and Honour,' the king, the Duke of York, and the Earl of Oxford gave their coronation suits.

[45] **Betterton, Thomas (1635?-1710):** He an actor dramatist and one of the most important theatre personalities of his time. Betterton was born in Tothill Street, Westminster. Following a mysterious and varied youth he eventually found his way to the stage. Following a performance in 1661 Samuel Pepys described him as *"the best actor in the world"* He died on 28th April 1710 and was buried in Westminster Abbey.

who represented the Duke of Burgundy, in the Lord Oxford's.[46]

It must, however, be confessed, that the Earl's dramatic pieces, though they happened to please our forefathers, will not bear the eye of a good judge; nor would be relished in the age we live. His Lordship, at his first setting out, most unluckily happened to stumble upon the design of writing a tragedy in rhyme, and meeting with better success than he really deserved, persevered in this error. By his writing in rhyme, it almost unavoidably happened, that his matter and expressions, in several parts of his plays, make a very mean figure in verse; and more especially to the jests of half-wits, and little critics, a sort of people, who never give any quarter: Besides this fatal error, in the first design of his plays, which has injured almost every scene, he has made no scruple, to leap over the bounds of probability, to represent the most notorious facts after a different manner than they are told in history; and most of his plays conclude without the least shadow of a moral.

But when I have said all this to the disadvantage of his dramatic pieces, (which perhaps is as much as the feverest critic can say with reason,) I must do them the justice, to add, that there are lines in them, of which no writer need be ashamed: That they are full of the highest and sublimest notions of friendship, love and honour; and that it is impossible for a discerning reader to peruse them, without conceiving an high idea of the real worth and merit of their author. His versification is, generally speaking, much better than that of most writers who were his contemporaries. The greatest part of these plays were written at the particular request of his Royal Master.

I confess, I am no great friend to heroic rants, and romantic notions; yet I am afraid, that in the present age, under the pretence of exploding whatever is romantic, we have laughed virtue herself out of

---

[46] **Oxford, Robert Harley, 9th Earl (1661-1724)**, He was the son of Sir Edward Harley (1624-1700), a prominent landowner in Herefordshire. Harley was born in Bow Street, Covent Garden, London, on the 5th of December 1661. He supported the cause of William III and was elected to Parliament in 1689 where he served until his elevation to the peerage in 1711. He became Speaker of the House and in 1703 made use of Daniel Defoe's skills as a political writer. Gaining from this experience, he subsequently used the talents of Swift in the production of many pamphlets against his opponents in politics. Involved in various intrigues he was forced to resign his posts in 1708 but later recovered his popularity and in 1710 became Chancellor of the Exchequer. The following year he became Earl of Oxford and Mortimer; and on the 29th of May he was created Lord Treasurer. Perceived to be in sympathy with the Jacobite cause he dallied and on 27th of July 1714 he resigned as Lord Treasurer. On the accession of George I. he retired, but a few months later he was impeached and and was committed to the Tower on the 16th of July 1715. After an imprisonment of nearly two years he was released in July 1717. Oxford died in London on the 21st of May 1724

countenance; and that love, honour, and friendship, resenting the unworthy treatment they have met with among us, have left an island in which they formerly appeared with so much lustre.

The Earl of Orrery wrote several poems besides his plays: He wrote a poem upon the King's restoration, which was well received, but which I never met with. He likewise wrote a political poem, entitled, *A dream*. In this piece he introduces the genius of France, persuading Charles the Second to promote the interest of that kingdom, and to act upon French principles. He afterwards introduced the ghost of his father, dissuading him from it; answering all the arguments the genius of France had urged; and proving to him, from his own misfortunes and tragical end, that a King's chief treasure, and only real strength, is the affections of his people. He showed this poem in manuscript to the King; upon whom, it is said, to have made a good deal of impression. The Earl, at his Majesty's request, permitted him to take a copy of it; but as it contained many bold truths, he gave nobody else the same liberty.

He was a noble patron to true merit, and lived in a state of friendship with the most eminent men for parts and learning. He had a particular affection for Mr. Cowley;[47] whose death, he passionately laments in a copy of verses, which is the first Dr. Sprat[48] has inserted before his edition of Mr. Cowley's works; and which I will lay before my readers, as a sample of the Earl of Orrery's poetry.

I shall make no scruple to say, that most of the thoughts in these verses are not only bold, but beautiful; and that his complaint, that a man's learning must die with him; and that he should be unable to bequeath to a friend, the most valuable of all his acquisitions, is extremely poetical and pathetic.

---

[47] **Cowley, Abraham (1618-1667)**: He was a precocious poet, a Royalist supporter and secretary to Queen Henrietta Maria and subsequently a Medical Doctor. Cowley's works include "Poetical Blossoms", "Naufragium" and "The Mistress". He was buried in Westminister Abbey but is now little read or regarded.

[48] **Sprat, Thomas (1636-1713)**; He was born in 1636, at Tallaton in Devonshire, the son of a clergyman; and following a non-descript primary education became a commoner of Wadham College in Oxford in 1651: and received his MA in 1657. He produced many works, the most notable being The History of the Royal Society, The Life of Cowley, The Answer to Sorbière, and The History of the rye-house Plot.

On the Death of Mr. Abraham Cowley, and his Burial in Westminster-Abbey

By Roger Boyle, Earl of Orrery.

ur wit, till Cowley did its lustre raise,
May be resembled to the first three days;
In which did shine only such streaks of light,
As serv'd but to distinguish day from night
But wit breaks forth in all that he has done,
Like light, when 'twas united to the sun.

The poets formerly did lie in wait
To rifle those whom they would imitate;
We watch'd to rob all strangers when they writ,
And learn'd their language, but to steal their wit.
He, from that need his country does redeem,
Since those who want, may be supply'd from him;
And foreign Nations now may borrow more
From Cowley, than we could from them before;
Who, though be condescended to admit
The Greeks and Romans for his guides in wit,
Yet he those ancient poets does pursue,
But as the Spaniards great Columbus do;
He taught them first to the new world to steer,
But they possess all that is precious there.

When first his spring of wit began to flow,
It rais'd in some, wonder and sorrow too;
That God had so much wit and knowledge lent,
And that they were not in his praises spent:
But those who in his Davideis look,
Find they his blossoms for his fruit mistook,
In diff'ring ages diff'rent muses shin'd;
His green did charm the sense, his ripe the mind;
Writing for Heav'n, he was inspir'd from thence,
And from his theme deriv'd his influence.
The Scriptures will no more the wicked fright,
His muse does make religion a delight.

Oh! How severely man is us'd by fate!
The covetous toil long for an estate;
And having got more than their life can spend,
They may bequeath it to a son or friend:
But learning (in which none can have a share,
Unless they climb to it by time and care;)
Learning, the truest wealth a man can have,
Does with the body perish in the grave:
To tenements of clay it is confin'd,
Though 'tis the noblest purchase of the mind:
Oh! Why can we thus leave our friend possess'd
Of all our acquisitions but the best!

Still, when we study Cowley, we lament,
That to the world he was no longer lent;
Who, like a lightning to our eyes was shown,
So bright he shin'd, and was so quickly gone:
Sure, he rejoyc'd to see his flame expire,
Since he himself cou'd not have rais'd it higher;
For when his wise poets can no higher fly,
They wou'd like saints, in the perfections die.

Though beauty some affection in him bred,
Yet only sacred learning he wou'd wed;
By which th'illustrious ofspring of his brain
Shall over wit's great empire ever reign:
His works shall live, when pyramids of pride
Shrink to such ashes as they long did bide.

That sacrilegious fire (which did last year
Level those piles which piety did rear,)
Dreaded near that majestic church to fly,
Where English kings and English poets lie.
It an awful distance, did expire;
Such power had sacred ashes o're that fire;
Such, as it durst not near that structure come,
Which fate had order'd to be Cowley's tomb:
And 'twill be still preserv'd by being so,
From what the rage of future flames can do:
Material fire dare's not that place infest
Where he, who had immortal flame, does rest.

There let his urn remain; for it was fit,
Amongst our Kings, to lay the king of wit;
By which the structure more renown'd will prove,
For that part bury'd than for all above.

The Earl, besides his poems, wrote a large romance in Folio, divided into six parts, and entitled, Parthenissa; of which, I will venture to say, that few, who can relish any romances, will dislike this. The Sixth and last part of it was written by the particular command of Henrietta-Maria, Duchess of Orleans, and Daughter to King Charles the First. To this princess it is dedicated; and the Earl begins his Dedication in the following words:

"*Madam,*

When I had last the honour to wait on your Royal Highness, you ordered me to write another part of Parthenissa; and you gave me leave at the same time to dedicate it to you.

Only your commands, Madam, could have made me undertake that work; and only your permission could have given me this confidence.

But since your Royal Highness appointed me to obey, it was proportionate to your goodness to protect me in my obedience, which this dedication will; for all my faults, in this book, cannot be so great as his, who shall condemn what has been written for you, and is, by your own allowance addressed to you"

Many of my readers will, I dare say be vexed to think, that the great man I am speaking of, spent his time in writing plays, poems, and romances, when he could have given us so good an account of the most remarkable transactions in his own time; in many of which he was himself engaged.

I must, in justice to his memory, acquaint the world, that he is not altogether so blameable in this respect as he appears to be. His chaplain assures us, his patron had drawn up a very curious account of what was done in the court or camp, in which he had any part, or could speak with certainty; and the public have great reason to lament they are deprived of those memoirs, which were either lost when the Earl died or suppressed for reasons not difficult to be guessed at.

Besides the pieces already mentioned, he wrote a thin folio, entitled, *The art of war*; which he had his Majesty's leave to dedicate to him. It appears by this treatise that he was well acquainted with the discipline of the ancient Greeks and Romans; and he proposes some things, which were evidently great amendments to the English military discipline used in his own time. In short, there are things in this book, which persons who have a military genius cannot but be pleased with; though the different arms soldiers carry at present, from what they did when the Earl was a General, make many of his observations less useful than at the time when they were first published. He dwells, for example, pretty long upon the great use of the lance or pike, two weapons, which are at present wholly laid aside; and compares the match-lock with the fire-lock, in order to prove the last the most useful.

The piece, which of all his writings, I confess, I am the most pleased with, and which I believe, is very fierce, is entitled, *An answer to a scandalous letter lately printed and subscribed, by Peter Walsh,*[49] *Procurator for the secular and Regular Popish Priests of Ireland.* His Lordship is so ingenious, as to insert at length before his own book the letter he answers, which is an artful piece. His answer to it is wrote with great spirit, in a very good style, for those times, and he appears to have been fully master of the subject he writes upon, and of all such facts as were necessary to support his cause. There is likewise a moderation in this piece, well-becoming a great man.

I shall give a final sample of what I have been saying

> *"Since I shall often have occasion (*says the Earl in the beginning of his answer) *to name Irish Papists, I have thought fit here, once for all, to declare, that I mean not thereby in all, or any part of my answer, any of those worthy persons of that nation and religion, who have still faithfully served the king, whose merit I highly respect; and the more, because it has been preserved from infection, even in a very pest-house; nor any of those, who having been truly sorrowful for having rebelled in the constancy of their subsequent services to his Majesty, have washed themselves clean; for I take a perfect delight in any change from bad to good; and I heartily wish, that every one of them had not so much endangered their being polluted again, as interceding and pleading for their guilty countrymen does amount unto. Having thus made this necessary digression, I shall now proceed.*

[49] **Walsh, Peter (1618?-1688):** He was born at Mooretown, Co. Kildare and became a a Franciscan. Based in Kilkenny he opposed Rinuccini. Walsh was one of the theologians who met at Waterford 'to examine the concessions and conditions granted by the Marquis of Ormond for the security of the catholic church and religion,' After Cromwell had taken Kilkenny, Walsh wandered until he finally settled in London in 1652. In 1660 he addressed a letter to Ormond in favour of fair dealing with the Irish Roman Catholics. This letter was published and drew a witty and vigorous but intemperate answer from Orrery. In 1662 Orrery's pamphlet, 'Irish Colours Displayed,' was answered by Walsh in 'Irish Colours Folded.' Walsh went to Ireland in August 1662, after Ormond had been installed as viceroy. He there presented him with "the loyal remonstrance" which he signed last as procurator of all the Irish clergy. When Ormond was recalled in 1669 Walsh retired to London, where he lived for the rest of his life. 'I confess,' said Ormond in 1680, 'I have never read over Walsh's "History of the Remonstrance," which is full of a sort of learning I have been little conversant in; but the doctrine is such as would cost him his life if he could be found where the pope has power' He died in London on 15th March 1688.

*The parts separate of this letter, are three. First, a preface,
secondly a petition, thirdly, a conclusion, or concluding with.
Peter Walsh, prefaceth, first, the fears and jealousies of those
whom he calls the Catholics of Ireland. Secondly, his own
affection to, and confidence in, His grace the Duke of Ormond.
Fears and jealousies are no less than must in reason be
expected in the generality of the Irish Papists; for though the
goodness and indulgence of the best of Kings may make their
condition safe, yet the conscience of their own guilt will never
suffer them to be secure. Pretended fears and jealousies were
the forerunners, if not the causes of troubles past. I hope, Peter
Walsh intends them not as such for troubles to come."*

The Earl wrote this answer to Mr. Walsh, when he was one of the
Lords Justices for the Government of Ireland, and Lord President of
the Province of Munster.

The last piece he composed is entitles *Poems on most of the festivals of
the Church*

His preface to this piece begins thus:

*"God, of his abundant mercy, having convinced me how much
precious time I have cast away on airy verses, I resolved to take
a final leave of that sort of poetry; and in some degree, to repair
the unhappiness and fault of what was past, to dedicate my
muse in the future entirely to sacred subjects"*

Though it is apparent from hence, that his Lordship's design was
very commendable, yet, as he began this work but the year before he
died, and in an ill state of health, it cannot be denied, that his poetry
in this his last composition, runs very low.

I find, indeed, that he composed most of his former pieces when he
vas confined by the gout; which made Mr. Dryden[50] tell him, that like
the Priestess of Apollo, he delivered his oracles always in torment; and
that the world was obliged to his misery for their delight.

---

[50] **Dryden, John (1631-1700)**: Poet, critic and cousin of Jonathan Swift.

This circumstance is, perhaps, the best excuse that can be made for his writing a romance: I am willing to think he wrote it to divert his pain, which might render him incapable of a severer study.

As during the wars he had ever been a zealous supporter of the Irish Protestants, in whose cause he so often drew his sword, he showed himself after the Restoration no less zealous for their interest, which he successfully defended, both in speaking and writing. The Irish Roman Catholics soon after his Majesty's return, presented a petition to him by Sir Nicholas Plunkett,[51] and others commissioned for that purpose, to desire they might be restored to their estates. This in effect, would have ruined the Protestants, who chose the Earl of Orrery, Mountrath, and six more, to oppose their adversaries before the King and his Council. The Irish Commissioners were so apprehensive of the Earl's eloquence and address upon this occasion, that Mr. Morrice assures us they came to him, and offered him eight thousand pounds in money, and to settle estates of seven thousand pounds per annum upon him and his heirs, if he would not appear against them at the Council-Board: But that the Earl rejected this proposal with a generous disdain, and told them, that since he had the honour to be employed by the Protestants, he would never have the baseness to betray them. This great cause was heard at length in a very solemn manner before the King and Council, where, when the Irish Commissioners had offered all they thought proper, and expatiated upon the loyalty of their principles, the Earl, after an handsome compliment to the King, boldly affirmed, that the Protestant subjects in Ireland were the first who formed an effectual party for restoring him; that the Irish had broke all the treaties which had been made with them; that they had fought against the authority, both of the late and present King, and had offered the Kingdom of Ireland both to the Pope, the King of Spain, and the King of France: Lastly to the great surprise, not only of the Irish, but of his own Brother Commissioners, he proved his assertions. By producing several original papers signed by the Irish Supreme Council, of which

---

[51] **Plunkett, Sir Nicholas (1601-1680):** Plunkett was an eminent barrister and M.P. for Meath in 1634 and 1635. Appointed Ambassador to Rome he spent much of his life in exile. In 1669 he was assigned to obtain from Charles II the restoration of estates of Irish Catholics. ("The Graces") He was married three times.

Sir Nicholas Plunket himself was one.

This last unexpected blow (for the Earl had concealed his chief strength, even from those with whom he acted) put an end to the dispute, in favour of the Protestants; and obliged his Majesty to dismiss the Irish Commissioners with some harsher expressions than he commonly made use of.

After the hearing was over, the Earl being pressed by his Brother Commissioners, to acquaint them how he came by those original papers, told them a formal story of their being found in the enemies quarters, and put into his hands by a person unknown to him. It is much more probable, that the Irish (among whom he constantly maintained several spies) were betrayed on this occasion, by some whom they imagined to be their friends.

Soon after this affair, his Lordship, with Sir Charles Coote, lately made Earl of Mountrath, and Sir Maurice Eustace,[52] were made Lords Justices for the Government of Ireland; and commissioned to call and hold a Parliament for the settlement of the Kingdom.

The Lord Orrery, some time before the meeting of the Parliament, drew up, with his own hand, that famous Act of settlement, which afterwards passed; in which he not only took care to establish the Protestant Interest, but that many Roman Catholics should be restored to their estates, whose behaviour seemed to merit that indulgence. When this act passed, it was looked upon as drawn up with great skill and address. Though the judges afterwards, by the partial interpretation they put upon it, gave too much reason for clamour and complaints. The Lord Orrery and his brothers, the Lords Justices, managed matters with so much dexterity in this parliament, which was held under their government, that all things passed in it as the King desired; and the Earl of Mountrath dying while the Parliament was prorogued, a new Commission was granted to the Lord Orrery, and Sir Maurice Eustace Chancellor of Ireland, to be the Lords Justices for that Kingdom.

Some time after this, the Duke of Ormond being declared Lord Lieutenant of Ireland, the Earl of Orrery went into Munster, of which

---

[52] **Eustace, Sir Maurice (1590-1665)** He became Speaker of the Irish House of Commons in 1639 and Lord Chancellor in 1660.

Province he was President. This was a post of great honour and trust: By virtue of it the Lord President heard and determined causes in a court called the Presidency-Court; and was in effect a Lord Chancellor for that Province. In this court he heard all matters that were brought before him with so much patience, condescension, and impartiality, would make use of so many stratagems to induce the contending parties to come to an amicable agreement, and employ his parts, interest, and authority, so effectually to this purpose, that he was justly looked upon by the gentlemen of the Province to be the very cement of that concord and union which was so remarkably observed among them.

He acquired so great a reputation in this his judicial capacity, that it is said, he was offered the seals both by the King and the Duke of York after the fall of the great Earl of Clarendon; but that his being much afflicted with the gout, prevented his accepting a post which demanded so constant an attendance.

He was extremely well, not only with the king, but the Duke of York; between whom he had the good fortune to make up several misunderstandings upon some points of a very delicate nature. The King frequently wrote to him: Mr. Morrice, his chaplain, tells us, he saw one of his majesty's letters, all written with his own hand. In this letter the King gave the Earl of Orrery many thanks for his great services, and particularly for settling things upon so good a foot in the Province of Munster; assuring him that in recompense of the pains he had taken, he was ready to oblige him in any thing he should desire. He then acquainted him that he was very well pleased with that part of the Black Prince he had sent him; and conjured him to go on and finish it. His Majesty concluded by telling him, in a facetious manner, that if he designed to defer going on with his play, till he was confined by the gout, he heartily wished him a good lusty fit of it.

The king and his ministers had so good an opinion of his judgment, that they sent for him more than once into England, to have his advice upon some affairs of importance.

His being a member of the English House of Commons, occasioned likewise his coming frequently to London; where he was constantly visited by men of parts and learning, and the most eminent bishops of the Church of England. As he always strictly adhered to the established church he was a great favourite with these; though he often took the liberty to tell them, that he thought them a little too stiff in some points; that he wished for nothing more than to see a union between the Church and the Dissenter; and conceived it highly barbarous to persecute men for any opinions which were not utterly inconsistent with the good of the state.

When the Bill of Exclusion was brought into the House of Commons against the Duke of York, he declared, that he could never consent to alter the succession; but that he thought it highly necessary to take care that neither our religion or liberties should be endangered, if the crown should happen to devolve upon a Roman Catholic. He was therefore for laying such restrictions, by an Act of Parliament, upon the Duke of York, if ever he happened to be King of England, as, in the opinion of several wise men since, would have put it out of the power of that prince to have oppressed his Protestant subjects; and have saved an immense quantity of blood and treasure, which has been expended to support the revolution.

It is well known, that both the King and Duke of York at that time would have consented to any Act of Parliament, and have submitted to any expedient (except the Bill of Exclusion) which could have been found out to make the people easy. The zealots for that bill imagined that they should at last force the King to comply with them; and therefore would hear of nothing but the Bill itself. By this their obstinacy, the King was drove to dissolve the Parliament; King James mounted the throne without any extraordinary restrictions upon him; and every Englishman knows, and has felt the consequences that followed.

The Earl of Orrery having being for many years afflicted with the gout, and for some time past in an ill state of health, died on the 16th of October, 1679 generally lamented by those who had the honour and happiness of his acquaintance; and leaving behind him the character of an able general, statesman, and writer.

It is, indeed, very apparent by his actions and writings, that he had a large portion of courage, prudence, wit, and learning. He seems to have been particularly happy in what we usually call a presence of mind; his parts and courage, whenever he was hardest pressed, afforded him unusual succours; and enabled him with a surprising dexterity to extricate himself from the greatest difficulties. We have seen him above being corrupted in the great cause between the Roman Catholics and Protestants; and upon another occasion, he refused four thousand pounds which Charles II who is known not to have been so delicate on this point, put into his own privy-purse. Mr. Morrice, who must know such particulars, affirms, that he was vastly generous to men of merit in distress, and charitable to the poor; for the benefit of whom he erected several schools and alms-houses. His natural parts were much improved by literature; and his wit and courage rendered still more amiable by his religion. He had a natural generosity in his temper: We have seen in what manner he employed his interest with the Protector; nor ought I to have omitted that, when Ireton had determined to destroy the men, women, and children, in the Irish Barony, who, after he had once pardoned them, had rebelled a second time, the then, Lord Broghill never left him, till he had persuaded him to lay aside so cruel a resolution. His person was of a middle size; well-shaped, and comely; his eyes had that life and quickness in them which is usually the sign of great and uncommon parts. His wit, his knowledge of the world, and his learning rendered his conversation highly entertaining and instructive.

The memoirs I am writing, would ill deserve the title I have given them, namely Memoirs of the family of the Boyles, if I should omit taking notice of the Honourable Robert Boyle Esq.; the seventh and youngest son of the Great Earl of Cork, and brother to the Earl of Orrery last mentioned.

This great man was born at Lismore in Ireland, on the 25th day of January 1627. He received his academical education at Leyden in Holland; and having afterwards travelled through France, Italy, and other countries, learned several languages, and made a great number of curious observations, he settled in England, and spent the last forty years of his life at the house of his sister the Lady Ranelagh. Having a plentiful fortune, and being eased from the trouble of house-keeping, and governing a family, by the care of that excellent woman his sister, he applied himself with so much diligence and success to the study of natural and mechanical philosophy, as has rendered his name famous, not only in England, but throughout all Europe; a great part of his philosophical works having being translated into Latin.

I believe I may truly venture to assert that no Philosopher, either before, or after him, ever made so great a number of curious and profitable experiments. He very rightly judged, that this was the only proper method to become a master of the secrets of nature; and there is one particular, for which he can never be too much admired or commended; it is evident that he made all his experiments without any design to confirm or establish any particular system. He is so much in earnest in his search after truth, that he is wholly indifferent where he finds it. We may truly say, that he has animated philosophy; and put in action what before was little better than a speculative science. He has shown that we inhabit a world, all the parts of which, are incessantly in action; that nature is every moment carrying on her grand scheme; and, that even our own bodies are affected by an infinite number of agents more than we imagined.

Without amusing us with barren notions, he lays before us the most important operations of nature herself; and, as a noble essay towards a complete history of her, has shown us the productions of foreign countries; the virtues of plants; ores, and minerals, and all the changes produced in them by different climates. In his *Statics, Pneumatics, and Hydrostatics*, he has shown the gravity of bodies in almost every medium; how far their motion depends upon their gravity; and demonstrated that there are such wonderful qualities in the air and water, as no Philosopher before him seems to have suspected. His observations and discoveries in the vegetable and animal world, are no less curious. He has rescued chemistry from the censures it had long lain under; and though the enthusiasts in this art, such as Stachenius, Helmont[53] and Paracelsus,[54] had made wise men almost out of love with this study, Mr. Boyle has shown of what infinite use it is to

---

[53] **Van Helmont, Jan Baptista (1577-1644):** He was born in Brussels and practiced as a medical doctor but is remembered as one of the founding fathers of Chemistry. He "investigated gases…and it was he who first applied the name gas (geist) to this family of substances….He was one of the first to recognize the role played by acid in the gastric juice" [The Catholic Encyclopedia]

[54] **Von Paracelsus, Theophrastus Philippus Aureolus Bombastus (1493-1541:** He was born in Switzerland and was one of the most famous Physicians of his time. He was also involved in the fields of Chemistry and Pharmacology.

philosophy, when kept within its proper bounds: That the particular qualities of bodies, such as their fluidity, volatility, fixedness, etc. do no ways so plainly appear, as from Chemical Experiments. His discoveries by the assistance of chemistry, thus rightly applied, have been so considerable, that the illustrious Sir Isaac Newton[55] himself, has thought proper to follow his example. Sir Isaac Newton, when, from the effects of bodies, he demonstrates their laws, actions, and powers, always brings Chemical Experiments for his vouchers.

The great Boerhaave,[56] allowed at present to be the first man in Europe of his profession justifies no less, by his own practice the use which our English philosopher made of Chemistry in Medicine; and has mentioned him with the utmost honour. Mr. Boyle has entirely destroyed several vulgar errors in philosophy. Nobody, I think, has dared to advance the chemical notion of substantial forms, since he has shown us the true origin of qualities in bodies; and the experiments made in his Pneumatic Engine, soon demonstrated the absurdity of that common notion, that nature abhorred a vacuum.

The gentleman, the merchant and the mechanic, are all obliged to him for several useful discoveries, which must render his memory dear to posterity. Instead of advancing abstracted speculations, he illustrates most of his principles by such experiments and matters of fact, as have turned to the profit and advantage of particular persons in their several trades and professions.

He has not only made many surprising and useful discoveries himself, but given hints, and laid the foundation for many more. By the help of these, some very valuable discoveries have been already made since his death: it is highly probable, that many more will be made; and that his reputation will rather increase, than diminish in future ages. The Air-pump was his invention: by the help of this engine, he himself solved a great number of phenomenas; and Sir Isaac Newton, and others have since made the most surprising discoveries. So that we may justly affirm, we owe no small part of the

---

55 **Newton, Isaac (1642-1727)**; Scientist and Member of the Royal Society.

56 **Boerhaave, Hermann (1668-1738):** He was born at Vorherr, Leyden and was one of the most influential surgeons of his era. He is particularly noted for his use of post mortems in the development of diagnostics. The most famous of his achievements in the diagnosis of esophageal rupture is now called "Boerhaave's syndrome"

New Philosophy to the this happy invention. So great was his modesty, (though in fact, he laid the foundation for most of the improvements which have been since made in natural and mechanical philosophy,) that he confesses, he has only drawn the outlines of science; and charges posterity to consider all his writings but as so many imperfect sketches. I do not remember, that he ever advances an hypothesis to solve a Phenomenon.

His beneficence towards mankind was carried to the highest degree. When with infinite application, pains, and expense, he had broke into the dark recesses of nature, and made many discoveries which he might have turned to his own profit and private advantage, he most generously made a present of all of them to his country. He has with great faithfulness given us an account of the processes of his laboratory; of his optical, hydrostatical and other experiments: I never yet heard any person doubt of his veracity in his accounts of these phenomena of which he was himself a witness. He has, I fear, with some justice, been blamed for believing many things too easily upon the credit of other people. It is probable, that as he abhorred to affirm what was false himself, he could not readily believe others capable of so mean a practice. It must likewise be confessed, that his style is far from being correct; that it is too wordy and prolix; and that though it is for the most part plain and easy, yet, that he has sometimes made use of harsh and antiquated expressions: yet under all these disadvantages, so curious is his matter, and so solid are his observations, that the hardest thing we can say of his most careless piece, is, that it appears like a beautiful woman in an undress.

Besides his philosophical works, Mr. Boyle has wrote several pieces of divinity: in these last, he is still more wordy, and makes use of more circumlocutions than in the former. To say the truth, I think his theological works, much inferior to his philosophical ones. It cannot however be denied, that he has often blended religion and philosophy happily enough together; and made each serve to illustrate and embellish the other.

Of all his theological treatises, that which I am most pleased with, is entitled, *Of the high veneration man's intellect owes to god.*

"Upon this occasion (says Mr. Boyle in the treatise) I shall take leave to declare, that 'tis not without some indignation, as well as wonder, that I see many men, and some of them Divines too, who little considering what God is, and what themselves are, presume to talk of him and his attributes as freely, and as unpremeditatedly, as if they were talking of a geometrical figure, or a mechanical engine. So that even the less presumptuous discourse as if the nature and perfections of that unparalleled Being were objects that their intellects can grasp; and scruple not to dogmatise about those abstruse subjects, as freely, as about other things, that are confessedly within the reach of human reason, or perhaps are to be found among the more familiar objects of sense.

The presumption and inconsiderateness of these men, may be manifested by several considerations:

———— It is probable, God may have divers attributes, and consequently, perfections, that are as yet unknown to us.

————————Though Philosophers have rationally deduced the power, wisdom, and goodness of God from those impresses of them, that he hath stamped upon divers of his visible works, yet since the Divine Attributes which the creatures point at, are those whereof themselves have some, though but imperfect participation or resemblance; and since the fecundity (if I may so speak) of the Divine Nature, is such, that its excellencies may be participated or represented in I know not how many ways; how can we be sure that so perfect and exuberant a Being may not have excellencies that it hath not expressed, or adumbrated in the visible world, or any parts of it that are known to us?

This will be the more easily granted, if we consider, that there are some of those Divine Attributes we do not know, which being relative to the creatures, could scarce, if at all, be discovered by such imperfect intellects as ours, save by the consideration of some things actually done by God. As supposing, that just before the foundations of the visible world were laid, the angels were not more knowing than man now are, they could scarce think that there was in God a power of *creating matter (which few, if any at all, of the Peripateticks, or Epicureans, to omit others of the ancient philosophers, seem ever to have dreamed of) and of producing in it local motion; especially considering the puzzling difficulties that attend the conception of the very nature and Being of the one, and of the other; and much less (as far as we can conjecture) could the angels spoken of, have known how the rational Soul and human body act upon one another. Whence it seems probable, that if God have made other worlds, or rather vortexes, than that which we live in, and are surrounded by, (as who can assure us that he hath not?) he may have displayed in some of the creatures that compose them, diverse attributes that we have not discovered by the help of those works of his that we are acquainted with."*

Mr. Boyle's supposition, that the Supreme Being may have several attributes and perfections, of which we cannot possible have the least notion or idea; and his illustrating this supposition by showing how improbable it is, that before the visible world was made, the angels themselves could have any notion of the Almighty's being able to create matter, and produce in it local motion; I say, this supposition, and his manner of illustrating it, does perhaps raise as high an idea in an human mind, as it can possibly conceive of that first mover, that cause of causes, whom we call God. I have, indeed, as well as Mr. Boyle, often heard, with horror and indignation, a vain creature, perhaps one of the weakest of his own weak species, talking in so positive and dogmatical a manner of the attributes, thoughts, and designs of his Creator, that one would almost imagine he had been one of the Almighty's Cabinet-Council

I have heard such assertions, from the pulpit, of such and such things being agreeable to, or inconsistent with, the Divine Nature, and of the necessity the Supreme Being lay under, to act after such or such a manner, that, according to my own way of thinking, I should have put the highest affront on the great Being of Beings, and been guilty of downright blasphemy, if I had aimed to persuade Mankind to a belief of such assertions.

Mr. Boyle, from his contemplating the works of nature, and reasoning after the manner I have just described, had formed to himself so high a notion of the Creator of the Universe, that he is said never to have mentioned the Name of God, even in common discourse, without making a pause after it.————- This proceeded from the high ideas which the word he pronounced raised in his mind, or, to use his own expression, from the veneration his intellect paid to God; and was agreeable to a precept I find laid down by himself in the following remarkable words:

"Whensoever we speak either to God, or of him, we ought to be inwardly affected, and in our outward expressions appear to be so, with the unmeasurable distance there is between a most perfect and omnipotent Creator, and a mere impotent creature."

The theological treatise, in which he has shown the least judgement, and the most invention, is, entitled, *Occasional Reflections*: The meanness of those subjects, upon which he makes these reflections, laid him open to the ridicule of a certain writer, who knows how to expose the least indecorum to the strongest colours. Mr. Boyle (though he meant well) observed too literally that precept of Seneca's *Omnibus rebus, omnibusque sermonibus, aliquid salutare miscendumest.*[57]

His diligence and application were almost incredible: One is surprised to think how a man could make with so much exactness such an infinite number of curious and useful experiments, and yet find time to study, not only the learned languages, but the rabbinical writings and oriental tongues; to look into every part of science, and compose such a number of different Treatises. I have myself seen no less than forty six distinct volumes of his writing; and, if I am not much mistaken, he published several others.

His philosophical and theological works are so well known, at least to the learned world, that I shall dwell no longer upon them. I shall rather choose to collect some of his maxims and notions, as I find them scattered up and down his works, upon three subjects; which, perhaps,

---

[57] "In all matters and in all discussions it is fitting to introduce something wholesome"

few people imagine he ever touched. The subjects, I mean are love, marriage, and Government.

Upon the two first of these, my pretty country-women will, I hope, excuse this great philosopher, if he talks with a little too much severity; especially when they are informed, that as he lived and died a bachelor, he had no opportunity of knowing by experience the charms and advantages, which (though I am likewise a bachelor, I do most steadfastly believe) are to be found in the conversation of an agreeable woman.

Of Love

"To undertake the cure of a lover, is, perhaps, the next weakness to the being one. I have, however, sometimes endeavoured to disabuse those servile souls, who being born to reason, so far degrade themselves, as to boast solely an excess of passion. A man must have low and narrow thoughts of happiness or misery, who can expect either from a woman's usage. I never deplore a man, who by losing his mistress, recovers himself. I venture to speak with the more freedom of love, since having never known the infelicities of this passion; but in the sufferings of others, what I say, will, I hope, pass for the production of my reason, not of my revenge.

A witty wench used to wish her lovers all good qualities but a good understanding; for that (says she) would soon make them out of love with me. I could wish (says he, writing to a friend, who had left a woman that used him ill,) that you owed your cure more to your reason, and less to your resentment; and that the extraction of your freedom was not a blemish to it. However, says he, I cannot but conclude, that your recovery, even on these terms, deserves I should congratulate you upon it. Your mistress has made you a much better return by restoring you your own heart, than she could have done by giving you hers in exchange for it. You have done extremely well, in resolving rather to become an instance of the power of reason, than of love; and to frustrate the vain hopes of your insulting mistress, who fancied her charms were sufficient to make you bear her usage.

To people in love, the felicity of two persons, is requisite to make one happy. Romances represent lovers so dexterously, that the reader admires, and envies their felicity; but I had much rather be free from pain, than able to talk eloquently about it. Few die of love; unless we may properly assert, that when love dethrones reason, though it leaves the lover alive, it destroys the man. Reason is born the sovereign of the passions; and though her supineness may sometimes permit their usurpations, she is seldom so entirely divested of her native power; but that, whenever she pleases to exert what she has left, she is able to recover all she has lost. Those who dote upon red and white, are incessantly perplex'd both by the uncertainty of their mistress's continuing kind, and of the lasting of her beauty.

A mistress's face often changes so much, as to make her lover wish inconstantly no fault; or that she had actually been guilty of it, that he might find and excuse for his own.

I am not, after all, an enemy to love, unless it be excessive, or ill placed.

Of Marriage

"Marriage is a lottery, in which there are many blanks to one prize. Marriage is a state which I can allow to others, much more easily than I can contract myself. I have so seldom seen a happy marriage, or men love their wives, as they do their mistresses, that I am far from wondering our law-givers should make marriage undesolvable to make it lasting. I can hardly disallow being moderately in love, without being injurious to marriage. The marriage of a wife Man, supposes as much love, as he is capable of, without forfeiting that title. Love is seldom confined, but by a match of his own making. A man of honour should try to fix his affections, wherever he engages his faith. Few but such as are in love beforehand with those they marry, prove so honest afterwards, as to be in love with none else. A

virtuous wife may love both her husbands friends, and her own, and yet love him with her whole heart. There is a peculiar unrivalled sort of love, which constitutes the true conjugal affection; which a virtuous wife reserves entirely for her husband, and which it would be criminal in her to harbour for any person.

Of Government

The art of Government is both noble and difficult; because a prince is to work upon free-agents; who may have private interests and designs, not only different from his, but repugnant to them. Wisdom alone can make authority obey'd with cheerfulness. The greatest prince's action ought not only to be regulated, but to be judged of by reason. A Monarch may command my life or fortune, but not my opinion: I cannot command this myself; it arises only from the nature of the thing I judge of. To think that all things done by men in power are done with wisdom, is too great an impossibility to be a duty. The being possessed of power, neither implies nor confers the skill to make a right use of it. A crown adorns the outside of an head, without enriching the inside of it. The jurisdiction of reason extends to thrones themselves. The splendour of a crown may dazzle the person who wears it; but will hardly impose upon a judicious beholder. It may be much questioned, whether the respect we pay to most princes, is grounded on our reason and inward thoughts; but though I see the folly of a prince never so great, I ought to pay him a decent respect. We may reverence authority in the weakest men; yet this is so difficult to do, that it is not often practised. We should use the fathers of our country as Noah's children did their sick father, who, when they saw his nakedness, covered it, being willing to see no more of it, than was necessary to hide it. The infelicities of declining states are not always due to the imprudence of rulers: the resentments of such imprudence, often occasion the highest disorders. Though the vulgar ought not too rashly judge of the actions of those in power; yet men of parts, who know their interests and designs, may judge of their counsels, and discover their errors. Affection and diligence in the service of the public, may, in spite of some miscarriages, prevent or lessen the ruin of a State. It is no breach of loyalty, to question the prudence of a Governor. Counsels capable of several circumstances, ought to be censured favourably. A throne not only affords temptations to vice, but engagements to virtue. Though so high a station may make a man giddy, it certainly ought to make him circumspect. A throne is so sublime a station, as must make a generous soul despise mean things. A generous mind must make a prince ambitious of glory; and this can never be attained but by great and good actions. The examples of princes influence strongly either to virtue, or vice; and the introducing good customs, is a much more noble prerogative, if rightly used, than to coin metals into money, and to make it currant. What a great account must princes one day give, who have such obligations upon them to be strictly just! And such a multitude of people committed to their care! Princes, who have any sense of shame or honour, will constantly remember, that there are too many eyes upon them to keep their faults secret, or themselves from censure."

The reputation Mr. Boyle had acquired among foreign nations before his death, was so great, that no strangers who came among us, and had any taste for learning or philosophy, left England without seeing him. He received them with a certain openness and humanity, which were peculiar to him; and when some of his friends have seemed to blame him for suffering himself to be so frequently interrupted by the visits of strangers, and condescending to answer all their queries, he has replied, that what he did was but gratitude, since he could not forget with how much humanity he himself had been received by learned strangers in foreign parts, and how much he should have been grieved, had they refused to satisfy his curiosity. His laboratory was constantly open to the curious, whom he permitted to see most of his processes.

It is true, he found out some things in the course of his experiments, which he looked upon himself obliged to conceal, for the good of mankind: Of this nature were several sorts of poisons, and a certain liquor, with which, he assures us, he could discharge all the writing of any deed upon paper or parchment, leave nothing but the parties names who signed it, and that the place from whence the first writing had been discharged, would bear ink again as well as ever.

King Charles the Second, King James, and King William, were so taken with his conversation, that they often used to talk with him with great familiarity. His four elder brothers being all noblemen, he was several times offered a Peerage, which he constantly refused to accept: Perhaps, notwithstanding all his modesty, he could not but be conscious, that his own personal merit had given him a higher rank in the world than any title the Crown could confer upon him. He likewise refused several eminent posts which were offered to him, both in the Church and State. Dr. Burnet[58] tells us, that *"though he had great notions of what human nature might be brought to, yet that he foresaw so many difficulties in the undertaking, that he withdrew himself early from Courts and Affairs, notwithstanding the distinction with which he was always used by our late Princes."* The doctor adds, that

> *"He had the principles of an Englishman, as well as of a Protestant, too deep in him to be corrupted, or to be cheated out of them; and that in these principles, he endeavoured to fortify all those with whom he much conversed."*

He made no scruple to condemn such public measures as he could not approve; but always did this in the style and language of a gentleman: Or, to make use of Dr. Burnet's words,

> *"He spoke of the Government even in times which he disliked, and upon occasions which he spared not to condemn, with an exactness of respect."*

---

[58] **Burnet, Gilbert (1643-1715):** He was born in Edinburgh on 18th September 1643. Following studies for the Church in Scotland he visited England and became acquainted with notable scholars including Boyle. Burnet was a precocious and ambitious clergyman and upon the introduction of Robert Moray, he became a member of the Royal Society. Strongly ascetic and Presbyterian in style, he published his "Memoirs of the Dukes of Hamilton," in 1676 and in 1687 an account of his travels, in a series of letters addressed to Robert Boyle. He opposed the Stuarts and actively supported the cause of William of Orange. He landed with William at Torbay, the place apparently being chosen at his instigation. Burnet was soon rewarded by the Bishopric of Salisbury and was chosen to preach the coronation sermon. He died on 17th March 1715.

The experiments he was constantly making in Natural Philosophy, gave him opportunities, which he embraced with pleasure, of employing a great number of people; and though by the many discoveries he made, he might have greatly increased his own private fortune, he could never be persuaded to think of doing so. All the noble medicines he compounded in his laboratory, were distributed gratis by his sister, and other persons, to whose care he committed them.

As he had a plentiful estate, despised pomp, and scorned to hoard up any part of his yearly income, his bounty to learned men in narrow circumstances were very great, but without ostentation. He presented one gentleman with five hundred pounds, who translated a small treatise which he imagined would do good. Mr. Collier and Dr. Burnet, who were both intimately acquainted with him, assure us, that he gave away every year above one thousand pounds. He was likewise a noble benefactor to the Royal Society, of which he was a Fellow. In a word, with a most uncommon and a God-like generosity, he devoted his time, his fortune, and himself, to the service and benefit of Mankind. His health was extremely tender, and his eyes weak; yet by living under an exact regimen, and never indulging his appetite, he attained to the sixty-fourth year of his age, and preserved his sight to the last. His head, which is prefixed to several of his works, is extremely like him. His fame still lives in every nation in Europe, and must doubtless give a just and rational pleasure to every branch of that noble family, who have the honour to be related to him.

The great Mr. Boyle last mentioned, had the pleasure to foresee, and the judgement to foretell, that the honour and reputation of his family would in all probability, be kept up by two of his nephews, namely, Henry late Lord Carleton, and Charles late Earl of Orrery; both of whom we proceed to give an account.

The Honourable Henry Boyle Esq; who was created Lord Carleton in the year 1714, was the youngest son of Lord Charles Clifford. He was naturally endowed with great prudence, and a winning address. Being elected a Member of the English House of Commons, he soon distinguished himself so much in that Assembly, that he was made Chancellor of the Exchequer by King William, and was much in favour with that prince. He continued in this post till the 12th of February, 1708; at which time he was made one of the principal Secretaries of State by the late Queen. He was consequently one of the Ministry, when the reputation of England was carried to so great a height, and when she obtained so many signal advantages over her enemies.

Soon after the Battle of Blenheim, Mr. Boyle, then Chancellor of the Exchequer, was entreated by the Lord Godolphin,[59] to go to Mr. Addison, and desire him to write something that might transmit the memory of that glorious victory to posterity.

As I believe this story is not commonly known, and as I think it does honour to the late Lord Halifax, (whose memory I must ever love and respect,) I shall lay it before my readers.

Upon the arrival of the news of the victory of Blenheim, the Lord Treasurer Godolphin, in the fullness of his joy, meeting with the late Lord Halifax, told him, it was a pity the memory of such a victory should be ever forgot. He added, that he was pretty sure his Lordship, who was so distinguished a patron of Men of Letters, must know some person, whose pen was capable of doing justice to the action. My Lord Halifax replied, that he did indeed know such a person; but would not desire him to write upon the subject his Lordship had mentioned. The Lord Treasurer entreating to know the reason of so unkind a resolution, Lord Halifax briskly told him, that he had long with indignation observed, that while too many fools and blockheads were maintained in their pride and luxury, at the expense of the public, such men as were really an honour to their country, and to the age they lived in, were shamefully suffered to languish in obscurity: That, for his own part, he would never desire any gentleman of parts and learning to employ his time in celebrating a Ministry, who had neither the justice or generosity to make it worth his while. The Lord Treasurer calmly replied, that he would seriously consider of what his Lordship had said, and endeavour to give no occasion for such reproaches for the future; but that in the present case, he took it upon himself to promise, that any gentleman whom his Lordship should

---

[59] **Godolphin, Lord Sidney (1645-1712);** He was a British Politician who was a major force after the revolution of 1688. Godolphin supported the Duke of Marlborough and acted on two occasions as Lord Treasurer. He was also a seminal figure in the development of the Racehorse industry.

name to him as a person capable of celebrating the late action, should find it worth his while to exert his genius on that subject. The Lord Halifax, upon this encouragement, named Mr. Addison; but insisted that the Lord Treasurer himself should send to him. His Lordship promised to do so; and accordingly desired Mr. Boyle to go to him. Mr. Addison, who was at that time but indifferently lodged, was surprised the next morning with a visit from the Chancellor of the Exchequer; who, after having acquainted him with his business, added, that the Lord Treasurer, to encourage him to enter upon his subject, had already made him one of the Commissioners of Appeals; but entreated him to look upon that post only as an earnest of something more considerable. In short, the Chancellor said so many obliging things, and in so graceful a manner, as gave Mr. Addison the utmost spirit and encouragement to begin that poem, which he afterward published, and entitled, The Campaign: A poem equal to the action it celebrates; and in which that presence of mind, for which the late Duke of Marlborough was so remarkable in a Day of Battle, is illustrated by a nobler simile than any to be found in Homer or Virgil. The Lord Treasurer kept the promise he had made by Mr. Boyle; and Mr. Addison, soon after the publication of his poem, was preferred to a considerable post.

Upon his late Majesty's accession to the Crown, in the year 1714, Mr. Boyle was created Lord Carleton, and was after made Lord President of the Council. He died a bachelor on the 14th of March 1725. His death was perhaps a much greater loss to his country, than was generally conceived; for I have the strongest reasons to say, that he formed a scheme, which he was not without hopes of putting in execution, and which, had it taken effect, would have prevented several calamities which this nation has lately felt.

His being long conversant in public affairs, had given him great knowledge in business: He frequently spoke in the House of Commons; and though many there were more eloquent than himself, I have heard it asserted by very good judges, that the late Lord Carleton was never once known to say an imprudent thing in a public debate, or to hurt the cause he engaged in: And I have heard the same persons add, that this was more than they could say of any one speaker besides himself in the whole house.

Having taken notice of four Boyles, more eminent men than perhaps any other family in Great Britain has produced within the same number of years, I proceed to say something of the late Lord Orrery.

Charles, late Earl of Orrery, was born in August in the year 1676. He was grandson to Roger Earl of Orrery, so often mentioned, and second son to Roger Earl of Orrery, an amiable good-natured Nobleman, whose parts placed him neither below, nor above the generality of mankind. Upon his father's death, the honour and estate came to his elder brother Lionel: This gentleman was a pleasant companion, drank hard, and died without issue on the 23rd of August, 1703.

The last Lord Orrery received his academical education at Christ-Church in Oxford, and had for his tutors Dr. Atterbury the late Bishop of Rochester,[60] and the Reverend Dr. Friend. I have been assured by an honourable person, who was his Fellow-Pupil, and lived ever afterwards in great intimacy with him, that he applied himself so closely to his studies, as made all his friends apprehend that he would injure his constitution, which was none of the strongest. Their remonstrances to him upon this occasion had no effect. Dr. Aldrich,[61] the head of that Learned Society, of which Mr. Boyle was a member, observing his uncommon application and thirst after learning, conceived a very particular esteem for him, and drew up for his use that compendium of logic, which is now read at Christ-Church, and in which he calls him, Magnum adis nostrae ornamentum, The great ornament of our college.

The first thing he published, while he was a student at Christ-Church, was a translation of the Life of Lysander,[62] as it now stands in our English Plutarch's Lives.

---

[60] **Atterbury, Francis (1662-1732)**: Bishop of Rochester he was born at Milton or Middleton Keynes in Buckinghamshire. He went to Oxford and on his graduation he continued to reside at Oxford, taking part in the tutorial work at Christ Church, and acting as a sort of right-hand man to Dean Aldrich. Atterbury was a crucial figure in the "Battle of the Books" and was also involved in the Jacobite plots.

[61] **Aldrich, Henry (1647-1710)**: He was born at Westminster in 1647, and educated at Westminster School He graduated with a B.A. 1666, and an M.A. 1669. He became Vice-chancellor of Oxford in 1692. 'In 1693 he requested Charles Boyle to edit the 'Epistles of Phalaris,' which had been brought into notice by a passage in one of Temple's essays. The publication led to the controversy with Bentley, carried on by the Christ Church wits, though it does not appear what, if any, part was taken by Aldrich." (DNB). He died unmarried 14th December 1710. He was noted as a Divine and Scholar.

[62] **Lysander** was a Greek legendary figure who is said to have died c.395B.C.

Dr. Aldrich, the Dean of Christ-Church, who was continually putting the gentlemen under his care upon such works as were a credit to the Society, finding the late Lord Orrery, then Mr. Boyle, was a good Grecian, desired him to put out a new edition of the Epistles of Phalaris.[63] The Dean probably thought that he could not have pitched upon any ancient author, more likely to inspire a young man of quality with sentiments agreeable to his birth and fortune.

Mr. Boyle, who looked upon a request from the Head of his college as a fort of command, readily set about the work that was proposed to him; upon which, when he had taken a great deal of pains, he put out a very fine edition of Phalaris, which he dedicated to the Dean, and translated the Greek text into Latin. His Latin style is classical and nervous, and has a certain spirit in it, which comes extremely near to the Greek original.

Towards the end of his preface, where he is giving some account of the edition he published, he has the following words.

Collatas etiam, (viz. Epistolas) curavi usque ad Epist.40.cum Manuscripto in Bibliotheca Regia, cujus mihi Copiam ulteriorem Bibliothecarius pro singulari sua humanitate negavit.

I likewise gave orders (says he) to have the Epistles collated with the manuscript in the King's Library; but my collator was prevented from going beyond the fortieth Epistle by the singular humanity of the Library-Keeper, who refused to let me have the further use of the manuscript.

Dr. Bentley,[64] the King's Library-Keeper, thought himself so much injured and affronted by the words last quoted, that he resolved to do himself justice, and to chastise Mr. Boyle in print: About two years and half, therefore, after the publication of Mr. Boyle's edition of Phalaris, the doctor published a laboured piece entitled, *A dissertation upon the*

---

[63] **Phalaris (c.570-554B.C.):** He was ruler and tyrant of Sicily being infamous for his cruelty. Phalaris is particularly remembered for his use of a brazen bull to burn his victims alive. Appendix I details the background to the significance of this figure.

[64] **Bentley, Richard, (1662-1742):** He was a renowned classical scholar and critic. He played a vital role in the improvement of standards of textual criticism. Bentley's criticism of the "Epistles of Phalaris" was his seminal work and led to the production of Swift's "Battle of the Books" Bentley delivered the first Boyle Lecture in 1692.

Epistles of Phalaris. In this dissertation the doctor denied the fact relating to himself, which Mr. Boyle had asserted; but not content with this, he attempted to prove, that the edition of Phalaris, published by Mr. Boyle, was a faulty and a foolish one; though he insinuated at the same time, that bad as it was, it was not Mr. Boyles. He went still farther: He took upon him to assert, that the Epistles which had been ascribed to Phalaris for so many ages past were spurious, and the production of some sophist; that they were nothing more than a fardel[65] of common places, and such an heap of insipid lifeless stuff, that no man of sense and learning would have troubled the world with a new edition of them.

The doctor's dissertation gave occasion to the famous reply of the late Lord Orrery's, entitled, *Dr. Bentley's Dissertation on the Epistles of Phalaris examined*; a book commonly known by the title of Boyle against Bentley. The dispute between these two gentlemen, whether the Epistles of Phalaris were genuine, or not, gave occasion to so many books and pamphlets, and has made so much noise in the world, that I believe there are few men in England who have not heard of it. I shall therefore endeavour to give such of my readers as do not understand Greek, not only a pretty clear notion of the nature of this controversy, but to lay it before them in such a light, that they shall be no ill judges of it. In order to this, it is proper that I should make them a little acquainted with the famous Phalaris, the Sicilian tyrant.

We are told, that Phalaris was a native of Astypalaea, a city of Crete; where, when he was very young, having made an unsuccessful attempt to usurp the Government, he was banished out of Crete. He retired from the island of Crete to Agrigentum, a city of Sicily; and soon made himself beloved and respected by all the inhabitants. Having an immoderate ambition, and resolving to be the first man in whatever country he lived, he persuaded the Agrigentines to make him the Overseer of their public buildings. In this post he hired a great number of mercenaries and workmen, all sturdy fellows, who depended upon him for their bread. At the head of these men, armed most of them with their axes, and other tools, he fell unexpectedly

---

[65] **Fardel** is an archaic word meaning bundle, a pack or a burden

upon the people of Agrigentum; and having killed such citizens as he chiefly feared would oppose him, usurped the Government, and reigned, according to Eusebius, eight and twenty years.

Having acquired his power by force and blood, he was obliged to maintain himself in it by the same methods, and to put a great number of people to death, who were daily conspiring against him: So that he is represented, by most authors, as a cruel and bloody tyrant. They confess themselves, however, not a little pleased with his behaviour upon the following occasion.

Perillus, a celebrated Athenian Statuary, had presented him with several pieces of his workmanship, and received a noble reward for each of them. At last, he brought him a bull made of brass, and somewhat bigger than life. When the tyrant had highly applauded the workmanship of this statue, Perillus told him, that he did not as yet know half the value of it: Having spoke thus, he opened a door in the side of it, and showed the tyrant that it was hollow, and big enough to contain a man. He added, that if a man was shut up in it, and a gentle fire kindled under it, the groans, which so exquisite a torture would force from the dying wretch, would be so modulated by a small pipe, that they would exactly resemble the bellowing of a bull. Phalaris surprised at so inhuman an invention, immediately ordered his guards to make the first experiment upon the statuary himself; which was done accordingly.

All Greece was pleased at the relation of this story; and Phalaris was universally applauded for so exemplary a piece of justice: Tzetzes[66] goes so far, as to compliment him with the name of Aristides upon this occasion.

It appears, from the accounts we have of Phalaris, that he was a man of vast abilities, great personal courage, and a noble soul: That he was a most excellent friend, as well as a most active enemy. His generosity to men of real merit and learning, was without bounds: So great was his esteem and affection for such men, that their opposing him in the most violent manner, could not induce him to hurt them,

---

[66] **Tzetzes, John (12th century AD)** : He was a didactic poet and scholar who preserved much valuable information from ancient Greek literature and scholarship.

when he had them in his power. Ambition (a disease which has tainted the noblest minds), seems to have been his only fault; yet in mitigation even of this fault, his actions almost demonstrate what he himself asserts, namely, that he only aimed at dominion, that he might have it in his power to enrich and do good to men of real worth. When such men accepted his generous offers, he always looked upon himself as the person obliged. The many conspiracies formed against him, forced him, though much against his inclination, to shed a great deal of blood. He frequently laments the cruel necessity he lay under in this particular; and makes the same excuse for his conduct, which Virgil puts into the mouth of Dido.[67]

Res dura, & Regni novitas me talia cogunt Moliri.[68]

The Greeks had so strong an aversion to Monarchy, or Kingly Government, that they branded all kings with the odious name of tyrants: and we cannot much wonder that the Agrigentines were uneasy under the Government of Phalaris, if what Pliny[69] says is true, namely, that he was the first tyrant the world saw.

His great genius, however, surmounted all difficulties. He not only reigned many years in Agrigentum, a city, which is said to have contained eight hundred thousand inhabitants, but conquered the Sicani,[70] the Leontines,[71] the Tauromenites,[72] and the Zanclaeans;[73] and according to Suidas,[74] made himself master of all Sicily. In a word, if cruelty, with which his name is branded in history, was his fault, we have seen many princes since his time, guilty of the same crime, in the meanest degrees of it, without being masters of any one of those great

---

[67] **Dido** was Queen of Carthage and has been studied in the works of Virgil, Shakespeare and Marlowe.

[68] "Tough business and newness of the Kingdom force me to contrive such things"

[69] **Pliny [The Elder] (23-79 A.D.)** He was a Roman author and politician.

[70] **Sicani:** According to the Greeks the aboriginal inhabitants of Western Sicily, as opposed to the Siculi of Eastern Sicily.

[71] The **Leontines** were a native people of the Ionian area of Greece

[72] **Tauromenium** was a city in eastern Sicily. It was founded c392B.C. by Dionysius I. Andrmachus became tyrant in 358 but the city was subsequently controlled by the Syracusians. It then passed to Roman control.

[73] **Zancleans:** The people of the city of Zancle in Sicily better known as Messina.

[74] **Suidas** was a Greek lexicographer credited with the preservation of much early writing. He lived circa 970 A.D.

and noble qualities, which Phalaris, even by the confession of his enemies, was allowed to possess.

The Epistles, to which his name is prefixed, were looked upon as genuine by the Ancients; who (to use Dr. Bentley's own words,) *"Ascribed them to the tyrant whose livery they wear. So that* (as the doctor farther tells us) *they have the general warrant and certificate for this last thousand years before the restoration of learning."*

They have been highly admired both by the Ancients and Moderns; who thought the style in which they were written, was strong and nervous; and fancied they saw in them the starts of a mind truly great, and some of the most generous sentiments that ever entered into the heart of man, though a little stained and discoloured with that insolence and fierceness which ware   natural to a tyrant and a usurper. Suidas speaking of these letters, calls them

$$\text{'E}\pi\iota\varsigma o\lambda\grave{\alpha}s \ \vartheta\alpha\upsilon\mu\alpha\sigma\acute{\iota}\alpha s \ \pi\acute{\alpha}\nu\upsilon$$

Most admirable Epistles! Stobaeus[75] and Photius[76] highly esteem them; the latter prefers them to the Epistles of Plato, Aristotle, and Demosthenes.

Aretine[77] gives them the greatest encomiums, and speaks thus to the prince to whom he dedicates them:

"Perlege quaeso has Epistolas diligenter : ____*Invenies in Phalaride nullum simulatonis argumentum; invenies maximi animi virum, qui neminem formidet, neminem ad gratiam alloquatur; invenies apertae frontis hominem, qui quod animo, id etiam ore habere videatur, qui nullam boni viri opinionem aucupetur. Quippe qui & gloriam, & omnium adulationem recuset, atque contemnat : Vis in Deos, in patriam pietatis exemplum? Habes Phalarim, qui de Diis pie loquitur, & exul ad restituendam patriam atque ornandam pecunias elargitur. Vis*

---

[75]**Stobaeus** was a Greek writer who lived circa 500 A.D. and is credited with the transcription of large tracts of the work of earlier Greek writers thus ensuring their preservation.

[76] **Photius** was a Greek scholar who died in 891 A.D. and played an important role in the preservation of ancient Greek and other ancient writing.

[77] Leonard the Aretine: Classical author whose *History of the Wars between the Imperials and the Goths for the possession of Italy* was translated by Arthur Golding in 1563.

studiorum musarumque amatorem? Phalarim intuere, qui Stesichorum poetam inimicissimum captum a se musarum reverentia servaverit. Vis liberalitatem? Quem Phalaridi prapones? Neque enim quod non accipiat, sed quod a se munera non accipiantur, saepe conqueritur. Quis bene de se meritis gratior Phalaride, qui manifesto conjurationis crimine contra se deprehensum medici sui precibus condonavit? Quid quod pluribus sponte sua pepercit? Haec, & hujusmodi plura, quam dignissima principe in his Epistolis facile quivis potest intueri. Et quod firmissimum est veritatis argumentum, semper sibi constat. Neque enim fieri ullâ ratione potest, ut simulando quispiam eundem semper tenorem servet, ne affectu, & conscientia vel invitus animi ad morbos ostendendos nonnunquam trabatur. Ceterum his epistolis nihil gravius, acutius, pressius, (& grecorum & latinorum pace dixerim) in hoc scribendi genere invenies.”[78]

It is hardly possible to say any thing more to the advantage of any letters, or any Prince, than what is here said of Phalaris, and of his Epistles.

Sir William Temple[79] having observed, that some of the oldest authors were the best in their kinds, mentions Phalaris and Aesop in particular; and then speaks of the piece, entitled, The Epistles of Phalaris, in the following words:

---

[78] “Carefully read through these letters, I beg you. You will find in Phalaris no sham matter; you will find a very magnanimous man, afraid of none, never currying favour with anyone; you will find one of pleasant mien, who evidently says what he thinks, who is never out to gain the reputation of being a good man. Indeed he refuses not only approval, and all kinds of flattery, he despises it. Would you like a model of reverence for the Gods, and the Fatherland? You have Phalaris, who speaks becomingly of the Gods, and even when abroad (or in exile) is lavish with money to maintain and adorn the Fatherland. Would you like a lover of studies and of the Muses? Look to Phalaris who, out of reverence for the muses, spared the Greek poet, who was his very great enemy, when he captured him. Would you like [a case of] generosity? Who better than Phalaris? He often complains, not that he does not receive, but that his gifts are refused, who better deserves to think well of himself than Phalaris, who forgave the crime of clear conspiracy against himself, at the request of his doctor? And what of the frequent occasions when of his own accord he spared people? Such and much else of the sort so worthy of a prince, can anyone easily find in these letters. And, what is the strongest proof of [his] honesty, he is utterly consistent. Nor could it ever happen that mere pretence would enable one to keep ever even tenor and not be drawn away by desire and distinction sometime or other to displaying, however unwillingly, some unease. Moreover you will never find (with all due respects to Greek and Latin writers) anything more important or intelligent or impressive of this kind of writing than in these letters”

[79] **Temple, Sir William (1628-1699):** He was a distinguished statesman and author. He was born at Blackfriars in London in 1628, was the grandson of Sir William Temple (1555-1627) provost of Trinity College, Dublin, and formerly secretary to Sir Philip Sidney. After distinguished service in the diplomatic service he employed Jonathan Swift and became a central figure in “The Battle of the Books.”

"I think he must have but little skill in painting, that cannot find out this to be an original; such diversity of passions, upon such variety of actions, and passages of life and Government, such freedom of thought, such boldness of expression, such bounty to his friends, such scorn of his enemies, such honour of learned men, such esteem of good, such knowledge of life, such contempt of death, with such fierceness of nature, and cruelty of revenge, could never be represented, but by him that possessed them; and I esteem Lucian[80] to have been no more capable of writing, than of acting as Phalaris did. In all one writ, you find the scholar, or the sophist; and in all the other writ, the tyrant and the commander."

The Reverend and Learned Dr. Bentley is of a very different opinion from all those great men we have just mentioned: The doctor not only asserts, that these Epistles are spurious, but that this is apparent from their being such stuff, as Phalaris (of whose capacity he seems to have a tolerable opinion) could never write. The doctor assures us, that,

"It would be endless to show all the silliness and impertinency, in the matter of these Epistles; for take them in the whole bulk, (says he,) they are a fardel of common places, without either life or spirit, from action and circumstance. You feel by the emptiness and deadness of them, (says the doctor to his readers,) that you converse with some dreaming pedant with his elbow on his desk, not with an active ambitious tyrant, with his hand on his sword, commanding a million of subjects. All that takes or affects you, is a stiffness, and stateliness, and laboriousness of style; but as that is improper and unbecoming in all Epistles, so especially it is quite alien from the character of Phalaris, a man of business and dispatch."

---

[80] **Lucian (c.120-180A.D.):** He was a Greek rhetorician. He was born in Syria and traveled during his early life as a public lecturer in Asia Minor, Greece, Italy, and Gaul (France). Lucian eventually settled in Athens but also held an administrative post in Alexandria. His many lively satirical works attacking contemporary superstitions and religious fanaticism include *Dialogues of the Dead* and *Dialogues of Courtesans*.

It is certain that both Sir William Temple and the doctor have put the matter in dispute (namely, whether these letters are genuine, or not) upon the truest and most proper issue, by appealing to the letters themselves. If they come up to the character Sir William Temple has given us of them, every man of sense will, I believe, think them to be genuine, though a thousand specious arguments should be produced to prove they are not so. If on the other hand, they are such stuff as the doctor has represented them, all who know the character of Phalaris, will, I dare say allow them to be spurious, though they have passed for originals so many ages.

In order therefore to make all my readers who understand good sense, though they are no scholars, competent judges of the matter in dispute, I shall lay before them, some of the letters themselves.

I flatter myself, that though I should neither be able to come up to the spirit of the Greek original, nor to the Latin version of the late Lord Orrery, yet that my readers will discover beauties enough, even in my translation, to convince them, that these letters are not a fardel of folly and impertinence, nor were wrote by a dreaming pedant. I shall only premise, that (as all literal translations must highly injure their originals) I have been much more solicitous to preserve the spirit and sentiments of Phalaris, than his words. I have likewise made no scruple, for the sake of perspicuity, either to fling out, or insert, a word or short sentence.

Phalaris to Polistratus and Daiscus.

"Meet me in the field, and at the head of an army. I neither envy you the glory of that victory you have promised the Leontines, nor shall dissuade you one moment from endeavouring to obtain it."

To Axiochus.

"Some men value themselves upon their birth. In my opinion, nothing but virtue makes a man noble: Every thing else is the work of chance. A brave man, born of the obscurest parents, is himself alone of more value, than a long worthless race of kings and princes. A scoundrel descended from noble ancestors, is one degree below the dregs of mankind. Recommend thyself therefore to the Syracusians by thy own personal merit, not by the nobility of thy ancestors, which was long since lost in their degenerate offspring."

To Polignotus.[81]

I will trouble you no more, either with my letters, or presents; but then I must insist upon it, that you likewise forbear, for the future, either to praise or defend my conduct: Since you refuse to receive my presents, your behaviour condemns me more than all your eloquence can justify me. The wise are of opinion, there is no less difference between words and actions; than between a shadow and a substance."

To Evenus.

"When I first took thy son prisoner, I determined to put him to death. Upon second thoughts, I had rather punish thee, by permitting him to live, than stain my hands with the blood of so worthless a fellow. Farewell."

To Ariphaetes.

"Your actions deserve a nobler present than I now send you: Do not be too inquisitive about mine: The less there is said of them, the better."

To Aristomenes.[82]

"I conjure you not to be concerned at my having received several wounds in the late battle: I am obliged by your affection; yet believe me, my friend, though those wounds had like to have proved mortal, they gave me no manner of concern. I could, methinks, wish to fall in

---

[81] **Polignotus** was a Greek painter of the 5th Century B.C. noted for his mural paintings in the Painted Stoa of Athens which depicted the sack of Troy. While none of his work survivies it is described in detail by Pausanias.

[82] **Aristomenes** was a hero in the Messenian wars against the Spartans (c.685 B.C.). He carried on the war from his fortress of Ira but following the prolonged conflict and significant reverses he fled to Rhodes.

the field of battle. What death can be more worthy a brave man, than to breathe his last, while he is contending for victory in the cause of virtue?"

To Nicias.[83]

"You hate your son, for not being like you: Every body else loves him, for the same reason. Learn from hence, what the world thinks of each of you. Farewell."

To Nicaeus.

"I find my bull, and other engines of torture, give you no apprehensions: If they did, you would hardly act in such a manner, as renders it impossible for you to escape them."

To the Leontines.

"I send back your spy, whom I took, and might have put to death: I have spared him, to spare myself the trouble of finding out some other messenger, to inform you of the preparations I have made against you. This poor wretch, without being put to torture, has given me a full account of your circumstances: He tells me you are in want of every thing but fear and hunger; of these two, he assures me, you have a sufficient quantity."

To Demaratus.[84]

"You are surprised, I hear, at the cruel manner in which I have put Arsinus and Dorymenes to death: To increase your surprise, know, that they had been pardoned before, no less than three several times, by that bloody tyrant Phalaris."

---

[83] **Nicias** was an Athenian leader charged with an invasion of Syracuse but defeated and subsequently executed by the Syracusans in 413B.C.

[84] **Demaratus** was the Eurypontid King (c.515-491 B.C.) credited with foiling the invasion of Attica by King Clemenes.

To Paurolas.

"I have done whatever became a father: You are therefore inexcusable, if you are wanting in the duty of a son. I am told, you neglect your studies; for which I have often blamed you: If you refuse to do what I desire on this head, I have nothing else to ask of you. Yet know, my Paurolas, that if you will but gratify the ambition your father has to see you a man of letters, though I shall acknowledge it as a particular favour, the real advantage of it will rebound to your self."

To Paurolas.

"No, by all the Gods, my Paurolas, I do not think thee profuse or extravagant: Since thou hast so noble a soul, thou shalt not be able to find friends worthy of they bounties, so fast as I will supply thee with money. Where a young man has so great a mind, it would be a shame if fortune should not enable him to follow his generous inclinations. Make no scruple to ask me for whatever sums you want; I shall never deny my son a part of my riches, since it is for his sake that I am chiefly pleased I have acquired them. I am so far from blaming your bounties towards your friends, who, I hear, are men of merit, that I am highly pleased with your method of proceeding, and conjure you to continue it. You may depend, generous Paurolas, upon having whatever sums you ask of me. I think my self obliged to return you thanks for putting my money to so noble a use, and bless the Gods that I have such a son."

To Orsilochus.

"If (as you was pleased to tell the world) Pythagoras's refusing to come to me, though I had often entreated the favour, was a plain sign that he condemned my conduct; his being with me at present, is a demonstration, that he has no ill opinion of me. Be it known to thee, Orsilochus, that the great Pythagoras, that philosopher whose wisdom is so justly renowned through all Greece, has been at my court for these five months last past. I need not tell thee that such a man would not have vouchsafed to keep me company one hour, if he had not found something in my soul that resembled his own."

To Stesichorus[85]

"I am infinitely obliged to you for that poem upon Cleariste, which you composed at my request. The disposition of all its parts are extremely artful; and, in a word, the whole piece is excellent. This is not only my opinion, (who admire whatever Stesichorus writes;) it is the opinion of the best judges in Agrigentum, who heard it read. You have not only acquired the admiration of the present age, posterity must be charmed with the beauties of this composition. I therefore once more return you thanks, that at my request you have enriched the world with so valuable a treasure. As to what you are pleased to intimate in your letter, of your intention to say something about me in some future poem, I conjure you, by all the most sacred rights of hospitality, to lay aside this design: Say nothing about me, either good or bad; nor sully your Divine Odes with the name of the unhappy Phalaris. I know I am lost to fame; and though there is no honour upon earth I should so eagerly covet, as to made immortal by your verse, yet such are the unhappy prejudices the world has already conceived against me, that Stesichorus himself cannot oblige them to alter their opinion. Lay aside therefore a design, O my friend, which may ruin your own reputation, and can do me no real service.[86] 'Tis true, I derive from my Ancestors an unblemished name; but necessity, and my hard fate, have pushed me upon actions, which, Heaven knows, were contrary to my natural disposition, and which I am very far from pretending to justify. I am sensible, I am not a proper subject for Panegyric: If you, my friend, who know me better, have a more favourable opinion of me than the rest of the world, preserve an esteem for Phalaris in your heart; but do not mention his name in your Odes."

---

[85] **Stesichorus** was a lyric-poet, born in Hymera, a town in Sicily. He not only persuaded his own country men to make war upon the tyrant, but by his eloquence and address formed a confederacy against him of several other cities. Phalaris was so insensed at his behaviour, that he assured him in a letter, the Gods themselves should not prevent his getting him into his hands. In effect, he found means at last to make him his prisoner: Dionysius, of Halicarnassus, says, that Stesichorus had all the beauties both of Pindar and Simonides in his compositions; Horace and Quintilian commend his style and genius. .

[86] "I have flung into this letter of Phalaris a sentence, or two, out of some other of his Epistles upon the same subject."

To the Children of Stesichorus.

"What consolation is so proper for you, as to put you in mind of that father's virtue, whose death you lament? The heart of Stesichorus ought not to be attended with tears, but hymns. When I entreat you to lay aside your grief, it is because I do not think Stesichorus a proper object of it; such lamentations ought to be made when those men die, who did nothing in their life-time worthy of remembrance. This is not the case of Stesichorus, who spent so many years in the service of the muses; who has gained an immortal fame; and whose name will ever be dear to posterity. Behave yourselves, therefore, O illustrious offspring of Stesichorus, as becomes the children of such a father. Do not lament over him as a man, to whom the Himeraeans[87] have decreed the honours of a God. I think I knew him well enough to affirm, that he himself was far from repining at the approach of death; and that he bore it with the same constancy and strength of mind, as those heroes had done before him, whose names he has celebrated in his divine poems. When he fell into my hands, while he had reason to believe me his implacable enemy, he showed no signs of fear: On the contrary, he discovered more courage, if possible, when a prisoner and in chains, than when he met me in arms and in the field. Thus wisdom triumphed over power; and the poet disarmed the tyrant. After I had been at a vast experience, and taken infinite pains to get him into my hands, I no sooner had him in my power, than, as if I myself had been the captive, I could do nothing more than humbly entreat him to receive some marks of my esteem, and thank him, that he vouchsafed to accept of them. I am so far from thinking that he became my debtor upon this account, or for those twelve years which he lived after I released him, that I shall for ever acknowledge myself the obliged person. Your father's great example not only taught me constancy under the misfortunes of life, but how to despise death itself."

---

[87] **Himera:** It was a city on the northern coast of Sicily.

To the Daughters of Stesichorus.

The Tauromenites (in whose behalf, you say, your father, before he died, ordered you to write to me,) do not deserve any mercy. They made war upon me without the least provocation: But I can deny nothing to Stesichorus. The ransom-money they paid me for their prisoners, shall be returned as you desire. Though some people may look upon your father as dead, I shall never think him so; nor shall my resentments against the Tauromenites transport me so far, as to make me refuse Stesichorus whatever is in my power to grant. Though he may justly claim respect from all the world, he has a more particular right to it from me, who, among those numbers of men which a multitude of affairs have flung in my way, never observed a nobler soul than that which animated your illustrious father. I have ordered the Tauromenites money to be restored to them; and take the Gods to witness, that upon this occasion, I think I pay less honour to your father's memory, than I receive myself, by having it in my power to obey his commands."

To Philodemus.[88]

"You highly wrong me, Dear Philodemus, if you imagine I made vows for your safe return, that I might not loose the five talents I lent you. May the Gods confound me, if so mean a thought ever entered the breast of Phalaris: What I did, was upon no account but that of our mutual friendship. If you resolve no body but yourself shall give your daughter a fortune, you may look upon those five talents[89] to be as much your own, as any other money which you have in your hands. If I cannot persuade you to this, make up your daughter's fortune ten talents, and let her owe one half of it to her father, and the other to Phalaris. I am pleased to hear that Theano speaks of me with so much kindness and gratitude; and that, though she is now become a mother, she has not forgot who were her friends when she was a maid."

---

[88] **Philodemus (c.110-37B.C.):** He was a Greek philosopher and poet. He emigrated to Rome wrote erotic epigrams and was admired by Cicero, Horace and Ovid.

[89] "**The Attic Talent** was one hundred and eighty pounds in English money."

To Amphinomus.[90]

"When I make a present to a deserving man, I think I am much more obliged to him, than he is to me: Since therefore you have vouchsafed to accept of those things I sent you, do not look upon yourself as my debtor; but be assured that I am yours. Farewell."

Conclusion of a Letter to Agemortus.

"You have refused the sum in gold which I lately sent you; it seems you started at the sight of it, and would not touch that money which came from a tyrant[91] stained with blood. Believe me, Agemortus, you are too severe and cruel, if you do not pity the hard fate of the unhappy Phalaris: I aimed at power for no other reason, but that I might have an opportunity of obliging my friends : But when, by the favour of the Gods, I am now possessed of power, I find I have no friend left to oblige; you, who I once thought my friends, by not vouchsafing to share my fortune with me, have deprived me of the greatest satisfaction I proposed to myself amidst all the labours and hazards I endured. By refusing to accept by favours, you reduce me to the cruel necessity of bestowing those rewards which are alone due to virtue and merit, upon a worthless tribe of fools and flatterers."

I fancy my readers are by this time convinced, that the Epistles of Phalaris are not *A fardel of folly and Impertinence*; and that if they are dreams, they are rather the dreams of Jupiter, (as, if I mistake not, the Iliad has been called,) than the dreams of a pedant. Who can be unaffected with the nobleness of soul which every where appears in them! We see an absolute Monarch scorning to palliate even his own faults; and who, while he shows a fierce contempt for the vulgar and common herd of his enemies, is ready to pay the utmost tribute to uncommon merit wherever he discovers it! If we may form a judgment from the matter and sentiments of these Epistles, (which I must once

---

90 Amphinomus was the son of King Nisos and one of the suitors of Penelope and was killed by Odysseus.

91 The Greeks had such an aversion to Tyranny, that many of them would not accept even of a favour, nor receive the least obligation from a tyrant.

more add, is the best way of judging of them,) we have the strongest
reasons to believe they are genuine. It must be confessed the doctor
has produced some specious arguments to prove they are not so; he has
laboured this point with all his might, raised a terrible cloud of learned
dust, and flung a good deal of it in the eyes of his readers. His
strongest arguments against these Epistles being genuine, are his
chronological ones: But I am of opinion it may be plainly proved, that
the ancient heathen chronology is so very uncertain, that no man can
form a conclusive argument from it. If we should allow the doctor
(which, perhaps, after all, is the truth of the Case) that these Epistles
were written originally in Doric, and afterwards transdialected; and
that there are two or three spurious passages in them, which has
happened to most ancient authors; I say, if we should make the doctor
these concessions, I see no reason why the famous dispute between
him and the late Lord Orrery may not be compromised; and why
Phalaris may not still be allowed to be the author of those Epistles
which no man but himself seems capable of writing; and which the
Doctor owns have been ascribed to him by the Learned World for above
a thousand years together. It may be demonstrated, that these
Epistles were not written by Lucian, (to whom Politian[92] ascribes
them;) and, to give the doctor his due, I do not remember that he
asserts they were.

Having said thus much of the controversy itself, it cannot be
improper to take some notice of the manner in which it was handled.

The doctor's dissertation, as I have already observed, gave occasion
to the book published by the late Lord Orrery, entitled, *Doctor
Bentley's Dissertation on the Epistles of Phalaris examined.* I believe
no book of controversy, upon a point of learning, was ever published in
England which was more universally read and admired, or which,
indeed, more justly deserved to be so. Mr. Boyle not only showed a
world of reading, and that the doctor was mistaken in several points
of critical learning, but fell upon him with so much wit and humour,

---

[92] **Politian, [Angiolo De 'Ambrosini Da Monte Pulciano] (1454-1494):** He was an Italian Humanist, born at
Monte Pulciano in 1454 and he died at Florence in 1494. He became professor of Greek and Latin literature at
Florence from 1480.He brought many Greek and Latin classics to a modern audience through his translations. He
was also a poet of note.

rallied his dogmatical assertions in so smart, and yet in so genteel a manner, as flung an infinite deal of life and spirit into a controversy as dry and as insipid of itself, as a man could well have been engaged in.

The doctor was provoked by this reply to write again. His evil genius tempted him to aim at being as witty as his adversary: But as raillery is by no means the doctor's talent, this unfortunate attempt gave a new handle to the laughers, (no despicable party,) who, one and all, declared against him. In short, the doctor lost, and Mr. Boyle got a great deal of credit by this controversy: The world was pleased to see a young man of quality and fortune get the better of an old critic: He received numberless congratulations upon his victory; Doctor Garth,[93] in his poem, called, *The Dispensary*, which came out soon after, has the following lines:

> *"So diamonds take a lustre from their foil;*
> *And to a Bentley 'tis we owe a Boyle.*

The doctor had some Wags, who were his enemies even in Cambridge: They drew his picture in the hands of Phalaris's guards, who were putting him into their master's bull. And out of the doctor's mouth came a label with these words: *I had rather be roasted than Boyled.* Though I confess I am no great admirer of puns, yet nothing is more certain, than that this pun would have been highly applauded either at Rome or Athens.

The world is, generally speaking, ill-natured enough to give a man a push who is going down: The Doctor having been proved to have been mistaken in some things, his enemies would scarce allow him, from this time, to be right in anything. This was carrying the jest too far: the Doctor has certainly his merit in his way. It is evident, that he has taken indefatigable pains to understand thoroughly the Greek tongue; and that he has restored several corrupted passages in ancient authors, for which the learned world is obliged to him.

I ought not, perhaps, to omit, that so much learning, and so many

---

93 **Garth, Samuel 1661-1719**); Garth was born in Yorkshire and studied at Cambridge where he qualified as a Doctor. As well as his practice he soon became noted as a poet and his life is described in detail by Samuel Johnson. His work *"The dispensary"* was one of the most famous works of the period.

apposite quotations, appeared in Mr. Boyle's book, as raised a report, that he was assisted by a club of wits at Christ-Church. The excellent author of the Tale of the Tub hints at this, when, in his battle between the ancients and moderns, he ranges Sir William Temple and the late Lord Orrery on the side of the ancients, and speaking of the latter says:

"Boyle clad in a suit of armour which had been given him by all the Gods, Etc."

The Doctor had scattered some reflections here and there in his writings, which the gentlemen of Christ-Church thought they had reason to take amiss; nor will I venture to assert that no member or members of that College might furnish Mr. Boyle with some materials against his adversary; yet thus much I am obliged to say, in justice to the memory of the late Lord Orrery, that I have seen such papers and collections all written with his own hand, as have fully convinced me, that he was at least the author of the greatest part of that book to which his name is prefixed: the same style and spirit runs through the whole piece; so that it must have been formed, and put together by one hand; and I never yet heard any reason to doubt, but that hand was the late Earl of Orrery.

Besides his celebrated book against Dr. Bentley, he was the author of a comedy entitled *As you find it*. This play is full of wit: to say the truth, the fault of it is, that it has too much wit; a fault so seldom committed by any of our modern writers of plays, that his Lordship has the more reason to hope for pardon. I am, however, very serious, when I say, that his comedy has too much wit in it. The proper business of comedy ought to be humour, not wit: it must however be confessed, that where humour is wanting, (which it never ought to be in comedy,) its place is supplied by nothing so well as by wit: and if we reflect how many comedies have been written of late without either humour or wit, we shall not be disposed to be too severe upon a play, which is at least full of the last.

The Lord Orrery has likewise written two or three copies of verses, particularly a copy of verses to Dr. Garth upon his dispensary, and a prologue to one of Mr. Southerne's[94] plays: it must be confessed, that his Lordship's numbers are not so harmonious as those which appear in the best poems of the present age. In the late Lord Orrery's verses, we discover the man of sense, and the man of wit, but not the poet.

As soon as he left Christ-Church, he was chosen Member of Parliament for Huntingdon; and, perhaps, no young gentleman ever came into the House of Commons with a greater reputation for wit and learning. His election for Huntingdon was controverted, and a petition lodged against him: the following speech was found among his papers, and seems to have been spoke upon this occasion.

> *"Mr. Speaker,*
>
> *I shall always look upon it as a great unhappiness to fall under the displeasure of this House; but it would be more than ordinary unfortunate for me in this case, if I should be wounded by a shot that was particularly aimed at another. I will not at present enter into the whole mystery of this prosecution, but only assure you, upon very good grounds, that the violence of it comes from one that originally had no interest in the Borough, but what he had from the very same place that I have mine; and, I doubt, has no interest in it now, but what he has from a much worse cause.*
>
> *I shall not make many remarks upon the evidence on either side; every gentleman here will make some for himself, and very just ones, I don't question: but give me leave to observe, Sir, what I myself know in relation to the hero of the witnesses for the petitioner. When the election was almost over, I must own, he came into the court, and complained then as he has done now, that he had been beaten; and produced his disordered periwig as an evidence of it; but I heard no reason then, nor have I heard any since, to conclude, that either he or his periwig were any thing more than a little weather-beaten.*

---

[94] **Southerne, (Thomas 1660-1746)** He was born in the autumn of 1660 at Oxmantown, near Dublin, and educated at Trinity College. He entered military service and was promoted rapidly but his military prospects were ruined by the revolution of 1688. Southerne subsequently concentrated on literary pursuits. His play 'The Fatal Marriage, or the Innocent Adultery,' brought him literary fame and financial security. His 'Oroonoko, or the Royal Slave' (1696), was a huge success on Drury Lane. None of Southerne's later output bought similar recognition. He died on 22nd May 1746.

But, Sir, if he received any affront, he drew it upon himself, by being where it did not become him to be, and by doing what it did not become a justice of peace, a recorder, and a deputy-lieutenant to do: though, perhaps, as a lawyer, he may say, he was about his business; for, indeed, he was setting people together by the ears.

I think there can be no exception, Sir, to any of our witnesses; several of them are gentlemen of great repute and esteem: one of them particularly, has so great an interest there, that he might be, and, I think, fairly was chosen Knight of the Shire; and I believe he is the only gentleman in England, that had all the voices in a county, and was not elected.

I will not take up much more of your time, Sir; but upon the whole, must submit it to the Equity of this House, how far they will think it inconsistent with their order or privileges, that a gentleman, who has the ill fortune to be a Peer, and the good fortune to have a considerable estate about a Borough, a noble and an ancient seat just by it, and a firm, and a large interest in it, should give himself the trouble to appear there at election of one whom he is pleased to esteem his friend, and has the honour to be his relation. I must here, Sir, do the noble Peer the justice (who has been thus furiously arraigned) to observe, that out of respect to the orders of this Honourable House, he refused the compliment the Corporation offered him of being made a Burgess, and qualified to vote at elections; and for the rest of his conduct, I can answer, 'twas very different from what, by help of some industry, and more malice, it was generally represented about this town. Give me leave, Sir, to say that I know this noble Peer to be a gentleman of great honour, of a genteel and an easy temper, and far from being apt to insult others, or to be easily provoked himself: and if any thing has appeared here today that looks like contradiction to this character, it will not in the least alter my opinion; for, to deal plainly with some of the honest managers of this affair, I can't believe they would scruple to use the same means to procure witnesses, that they did to get votes."

This affair of the Huntingdon election, which was, perhaps, a little embittered by the foregoing speech, occasioned a duel between Mr. Boyle and Mr. W—-ly,[95] the gentleman who stood against him. They fought in Hyde-Park in a gravel pit, near the gate which now leads to Grosvenor-Square. Mr. Boyle received several wounds himself before he hurt his adversary; but at last making a resolute thrust, he wounded Mr. W—ly in such manner, a little above the thigh as made that gentleman desire the contest might proceed no farther. Mr. Boyle granted his request; but had like to have died by the several wounds he had received; and languished for many months after the duel.

He had contracted a particular intimacy and friendship with the late Colonel Codrington,[96] a gentleman eminent for his wit, his learning and his courage; and who sometime after his friendship had commenced with Mr. Boyle, was appointed Governor of Jamaica. The following speech, which was also found among the late Lord Orrery's papers, seems a pretty plain proof, that he was no less zealous in the defence of his absent friend, than of himself; a character not very common in the present age.

"*Mr. Speaker,*

I attended this committee; and all that appeared there considerable against Colonel Codrington, came from one who appeared plainly to be a prejudiced person; for he was at the same time, and for the same thing a witness here, and a petitioner in another place, against the Governor. His evidence, Sir, so frivolous and so absurd, and so much consisted either of hearsay, or of his own injuries, that I was of opinion it ought not to have been taken down; that when it was taken, it ought not to have been reported; and now it is reported, I am confident it cannot find credit with any gentleman, who will give himself the trouble to consider it impartially. 'Twas said publicly in the House, when the petition was brought in, (and I have reason to

---

95 Wortley, Francis (1692-: As far as I can ascertain this is the other duellist. He was the son of Sidney Wortley Montagu.

96 Codrington, Christopher, (1668-1710): Christiopher Codrington was in fact Governor of the Leeward Islands not Jamaica from May 1699 to February 1704.

believe some gentlemen were prepossessed with the opinion,) that Colonel Codrington had illegally got possession of an estate of two thousand pounds per annum; but I must appeal to the gentlemen who were of this Committee, if there was the least proof, nay, or the least insinuation offered touching any such thing; though the petitioner had all the fair play in the world, both to make out this, and all the rest of his charge; for he sought plainly against a gentleman, who had no weapons; he accused a man at a great distance, who is yet, in all probability, ignorant that there is any such accusation against him, and therefore could not instruct anybody to plead his cause; though it happened pretty luckily, that in everything alleged against him, either the trifling charge, or the weak proofs, were the strongest defence in the world for him.

But, Sir, I must say, with submission, that if anything had been made out against this gentleman, yet this House could not regularly now come to any resolution against him. This petitioner preferred a complaint, as he ought to do, to the King: his Majesty, referred the examination of the complaint to the Commissioners of Trade: they made their report of it; and according to that report, made an order in Council, which I have here. This order is as full, and as much to the advantage of the petitioner as he could reasonably desire; and therefore he ought not to have come here, till the Governor had refused to give a satisfactory answer to this order; and I am of opinion, that if the House had been fairly acquainted with the steps of this matter, they would not have received this petition. But certainly, Sir, for the House to do anything more in it now, is going out of the way, to do a particular hardship, if not injustice: 'Tis not only giving judgment, in my opinion, for a man that has proved nothing, but against a man that has not been heard.

But I hope, Sir, this gentleman's character, will at least defend him here, as well as everywhere else, from any unreasonable or unwarrantable severity: I may modestly say, he has as clear and as general a reputation as any man; and has done as much both at home and abroad to deserve it; and there is nobody that knows him, I dare say, but believes him to have too much honour to do any injustice, and too much sense to do anything that is ridiculous; and that he is much likelier both from his generosity, as well as his probity, to give away an estate, than to take one away. (I hope, Sir, what I have said will not be owing to partiality: I am very conscious to myself, that if I would have acted the part of a true friend, I should have been silent; but then I thought I should be wanting in my duty to this House, where, whilst I have the honour to sit, I shall look upon myself to be as much obliged to defend the innocent, as to prosecute the guilty.) The plain truth of this matter, is , Sir, that this gentleman has too much merit to be endured by those that have none; and I am very well assured, both from the character of his accuser, and his own, that he is really, and at the bottom more hated for his good qualities, than disliked for his management: his impartiality has drawn upon him the enmity of those who stood in need of his favour; and his integrity has exasperated those who could have lived much better by his corruption."

There is that happy turn and spirit in the two foregoing speeches, which seldom fail of taking in a public assembly; and which methinks, sufficiently show that the late Lord Orrery might, if he had pleased, have become an excellent speaker. It is, however, certain, that after he became a Member of the House of Lords, he never spoke in that assembly. What qualities must we therefore conceive requisite to form a Public Speaker? when we see such men as the late Earl of Orrery, the late Earl of Shaftsbury, the late Mr. Addison, Mr. Prior, and Mr. Mainwaring, sit silent; while ——- and ———— and —— and —- hold forth upon every subject that falls under debate?

Mr. Boyle's elder brother dying without issue, as I have already observed, in the year 1703, he became Earl of Orrery; and soon after married the Lady Elizabeth Cecil,[97] daughter of John Earl of Exeter.[98]

[97] **Cecil, Lady Elizabeth (d.1708)**: She was the daughter of John Cecil 5th Earl of Exeter. She married Charles Boyle on 30th March 1706 and died on 4th November 1708. She had one child, John afterwards Lord Orrery.

[98] **Cecil, John 5th Earl of Exeter (1648-1700)**; He was the son of John Cecil and Frances Manners and was born in 1648. He died on 29th August 1700.

This young lady, who had a great deal of beauty and merit, died within a few years after her marriage with the Lord Orrery. He loved her tenderly, always mentioned her name with great affection, and had by her that only son, who has lately succeeded to his honours and estate.

The late Queen Anne, who had abler Ministers about her, than any Prince who has wore the British Crown since Queen Elizabeth, and who knew the Lord Orrery's merit, took him into her Privy-Council, created him an English Peer, graced him with the Order of the Thistle, gave him a Regiment, and made him a Major-General of the Foot. He was present at the Battle of Taniers, which cost the English more blood than any in the last war; and (as I have been assured by an officer who served that day under him) led on his regiment with the utmost gallantry, in that part of the field where the action was hottest, and where most of his men fell on each side of him.

The late Queen who knew he was no less qualified for the Cabinet than the camp, made him likewise her Envoy Extraordinary to the States of Flanders and Brabant,[99] with an appointment of ten pounds per diem. In this employment he behaved with great dexterity; and though, as he has himself assured me, he never received a single farthing from the Treasury all the while he resided at Brussels, he maintained the dignity of his post in every respect, kept a most elegant table, and made himself universally loved and esteemed by those who had any transactions with him. He was in this post at a very delicate juncture, namely during the Treaty of Utrecht, when the inhabitants of Brussels knew very well, that they were soon to become the Emperor's subjects, and that the Queen of great Britain would have nothing more to do with them. Upon this occasion, and being also satisfied, that the Emperor was not upon good terms with Her Majesty, some of them, who were in authority, took the liberty to show less respect to her Minister than they had formerly done. The Earl of Orrery, who looked upon their behaviour as an indignity to the Crown of great Britain, managed with so much resolution and dexterity, that

---

[99] **Duchy of Brabant**: It was an area between the rivers Schelde (*Scheldt*) and Dijle. It was ruled by the Counts of Leuven (*Louvain*), who enlarged their domain considerably between the 10th and 12th centuries. In 1477 it came under Habsburg rule. Following Treaty of Westphalia the Duchy it lost most of its territory north of Antwerp to the Netherlands. Following a chequered period including rule by Napoleon the three parts were unified from 1814 to 1830, until the final separation of Belgium from the Netherlands in 1839.

when they thought his power was declining, or rather, that he had none at all, he got every one of them turned out of their posts.

Upon the late King's accession to the throne, the Earl of Orrery was not only continued in his command in the army, but made one of the Lords of his Majesty's Bed-Chamber, and Lord-Lieutenant of the County of Somerset.

He was induced to accept of these posts, by being made to hope that his Majesty would begin his reign with moderate measures; and that his Ministers, instead of advising him to act as a head of a party, would endeavour to make him the happy and beloved King of a powerful and united nation. His Lordship was inclined to believe, that this would be the case, from what was told him by some noblemen, with whom, at that time, he lived in a strict friendship; but more especially from what was said to him by the late Earl of Halifax. His Lordship and that able Minister, had always been upon as good terms as two persons could well be, who seldom voted on the same side in the House of Peers. It is well known, that the late Lord Halifax did, in effect, advise his Royal master to moderate measures at the beginning of his reign; but, that other people who were jealous of that Lord's power and great abilities, soon found out a method to lessen his credit at Court.

The first parliament under the late King opened with the impeachment of the Lord Oxford, and several others, who had been Ministers in the preceding reign: The Earl of Orrery, though he thought himself ill used by the Lord Oxford, (who, as I have already observed, never sent him any money while he resided in Brussels, and who had opposed his interest on another occasion,) yet could never be brought to vote against him. He thought him a luke-warm friend, and too dilatory in business; but at the same time was satisfied, that he was an incorrupt Minister, and wished well to his country.

There were several other occasions in which the Lord Orrery could not be persuaded to fall in with the violent humour of those times: He frequently voted against the Ministers: upon which it was confidently reported that he was to be removed from all his posts. This occasioned his absenting himself from the Court, a place, where a man who is thought falling, is seldom looked upon very kindly. His friends, however, assured him, that they had reasons to believe the King had a personal esteem for him, and earnestly persuaded him to appear at Court as usual. His Lordship was at last so much moved by what was said to him, that though he could not bring himself to go to Court he wrote a letter to his Majesty. I have been assured by a person of credit, who has seen this letter, that the contents of it were every way becoming an English Peer: that his Lordship told his Majesty, that though he looked upon his service as a high honour, yet that when he first entered into it, he did not conceive, it was expected from him, that he should vote against his conscience and his judgment: that he must confess, it was his misfortune to differ widely in opinion from some of his Majesty's Ministers; that if those gentlemen had represented this to his Majesty as a crime not to be forgiven, and his Majesty himself thought so, he was ready to resign those posts he enjoyed; from whence, he found he was already removed by common report, which was rather encouraged, than contradicted by the Ministers.

Whether it were, that this letter made some impression upon the King, or whether his Majesty had conceived before, a more than ordinary esteem for the Lord Orrery, he was not removed from his post so soon as he expected; though some other Lords lost their employments, with whom at this time he acted in concert.

His Majesty soon after went to Hanover; and while he was there, the Lord Orrery's Regiment was taken from him; though it is still a doubt, with some people, whether this was done with or without his Majesty's knowledge. However that be, his Lordship looking upon it as a mark of displeasure, resigned his post as Lord of the Bedchamber, to the no small joy of those who were no strangers to his engaging address and could not be easy, while they saw him in a station which gave so often access to the royal presence.

The Lord Orrery resigned his post in the bed-Chamber in the year 1716; and on 28th September, 1722 was committed close prisoner to the Tower, by warrant of a Committee, upon suspicion of high-treason, and being concerned in the plot, which is usually distinguished by the name of Layer's-Plot.[100] I shall give my readers some account of the treatment he met with upon this occasion, as I had it from his own

---

[100] **Layer, Christopher (1683-1723)**: Jacobite conspirator he was born on 12th of November 1683, and was the son of John Layer, laceman, of Durham Yard, Strand. He was executed at Tyburn on 17th of May 1723.

mouth, and from some persons who were about him, and who, I believe, would not deceive me.

The day before he was sent to the Tower, namely, on 27th of September, about seven in the morning, he was taken into custody, at his country house at Britwell, by a colonel of the army, who was sent down with a small party for that purpose, and followed by one of the Under-Secretaries. His Lordship's whole house, every bed in it, and all the pockets of his clothes and breeches, were thoroughly searched: all his private letters and papers were seized, and flung together into a large sack. His Lordship desired that his Will, which was sealed up, and endorsed, might not be broke open; but was not able to obtain this favour. On the same day and hour, when his own person was seized at Britwell, his secretary, who was at his house in town, and all his papers there, were likewise seized. His Lordship was brought up to town the same day he was taken into custody; none of his friends were suffered to see him. A Colonel lay on a couch by him, while an inferior Officer, and thirty-five soldiers, kept guard in his house all night. He was carried, and examined the next day before some Lords of the Council. Being ordered to withdraw after his examination, he thought he saw so plainly, by the questions which had been asked him, that nothing material could be charged upon him, that he was not under the least apprehensions of being sent to the Tower. He found himself mistaken: the lieutenant of the Tower came to him, and acquainted him, in an handsome manner, that he believed his lordship would lodge there that night. Being told at the same time, that there was no accommodations as yet fit for him, he entreated the Lords of the Council, that since he was kept from sleeping the night before, he might be permitted to repose himself under a sufficient guard for one night at his house in town. This was refused him. The present Earl of Orrery, whose filial piety can never be too much admired or praised, when he found his father was to be committed a close prisoner to the Tower, earnestly entreated to be shut up with him. But this favour was thought too considerable to be granted, either to the father or the son. The Earl was committed a close prisoner to the Tower, and none of his friends or nearest relatives suffered to have access to him. He had some years before been so ill, and was in so weak a condition at the Bath, that he was carried from one room to another in his servant's arms; and all about him despaired of his life: ever since that terrible sickness, his health had been extremely delicate: to say the truth, he had kept himself alive by nothing but a continual and regular exercise, being usually on horseback every day of his life about seven in the morning. Confinement, therefore, was looked upon by all his friends to be as certain, though a more painful death, to a man in such circumstances, than if his head had been immediately struck off upon Tower-Hill. The Earl under this rigorous confinement had no comforts, but what he drew from a clear conscience, an undaunted courage, and the consideration, that by the laws of his country, he must in a short time be delivered out of prison, or brought to his trial. This last consolation was soon taken from him: the parliament, which met on the 9th October, after his imprisonment, passed a bill to suspend the Habeas Corpus Act for one whole year; which had never been done before since the English were called a free people. It was not so much as proposed in the reign of the late Queen, when the Pretender was known to be on the coast of Scotland, with a considerable force; nor in the late King's reign, when the Earl of Mar[101] was at the head of a numerous army in Scotland, and when a body of the Pretender's friends were also in arms in this kingdom: yet this Act, the bulwark of the English liberties, was now suspended for the space of a whole year, upon Kit Layer's terrible plot, though not one man had appeared in arms, though not one drop of blood had been spilt, nor any of that party, who called themselves his Majesty's loyal subjects, been injured in their properties. The Bill which suspended the Habeas Corpus Act, bore so much the harder upon the Earl of Orrery, as by virtue of it he was still kept a prisoner, though he had been under confinement for sometime before the meeting of the Parliament. A Secretary of State desired the consent of the House of Peers, to

---

[101] **Erskine, John, (1675-1732)** sixth or eleventh Earl of Mar of the Erskine line 1675-1732. He was the eldest son of Charles, tenth earl of Mar. In 1713 he married Frances Pierrepoint, second daughter of the Duke of Kingston, and sister of Lady Mary Wortley Montagu. Erskine was a strong supporter of the Stuart cause and was one of the key leaders in the Bonnie Prince Charlie rebellion.

Following the defeat of the rebellion, he suggested a scheme to Atterbury, Bishop of Rochester apparently in order to betray the plot thus ingratiating himself with the Government. Atterbury expressed the general opinion regarding Mar, that 'it was impossible for him ever to play a fair game or to mean but one thing at once'. In 1725 he severed his connection with the Stuarts. Erskine lived in Paris until 1729, when he moved to Aix-la-Chapelle, where he died in May 1732.

detain the Earl of Orrery prisoner in the Tower, by virtue of the Act mentioned: to which the House consented. His Lordship thought he had reason to expect, from the strong professions of friendship, which some Lords, who were then well with the Ministers, had made him, that they could at least have articled for his Liberty. He found himself very much mistaken; and this affair taught him a certain lesson, which he never afterwards forgot.

His close confinement soon brought upon him a fit of sickness; his body languished, and his health was impaired every day, till at last he was reduced to such an extremity, that Dr. Mead[102] went boldly to the Council, and told them, that unless the Earl of Orrery was immediately set at Liberty, he would not answer for his life twenty four hours; and that if a purging should come upon him, he was satisfied it would carry him off in twelve hours. Upon this remonstrance, his Lordship was at last admitted to bail, after having been kept in the Tower about six months. The present Earl of Burlington, and the late Lord Carleton,[103] who could not think of suffering so near a relation, and so valuable a man to die in prison, readily entered into recognizance of twenty thousand pounds each, for his appearance, and his Lordship himself was bound in a recognizance of thirty thousand pounds more. Notwithstanding all this, the utmost favour he could obtain, was to be sent down to his house at Britwell, in custody of two officers, in whose company he was allowed to take the air.

When he first came out of the Tower, he was in so weak a condition, that if he walked, he was supported by two persons; and I, and many others, have often heard him say, that he never recovered his constitution again. His friends think they may justly impute his death, though it happened some time after, to this rigorous confinement, which he was forced to endure, though nothing like a crime was ever proved upon him.

---

[102] **Mead, Richard, M.D. (1673-1754)** He was the eleventh child of Matthew Mead, minister of Stepney, Middlesex and was born in that parish on 11th August 1673.

[103] **Boyle, Henry, Baron Carleton (d. 1725):** A politician he was the third and youngest son of Charles, Lord Clifford, of Lanesborough and grandson of Richard Boyle, second earl of Cork.

Since the death of this excellent person was, in all probability, hastened in the manner I have mentioned, I beg leave to say something of the suspension of the Habeas Corpus Act, and of the treatment of such as are called State Criminals.

The Habeas Corpus Act is allowed, on all hands, to be the greatest and strongest bulwark of the English liberties. It must, I think, be also admitted, that most ministers have had their piques and resentments against particular persons; and that no time is so likely for a minister to gratify his private revenge, under the mask of zeal for the public welfare, as when there is either some real or pretended plot. At such a time, (if the Habeas Corpus Act is suspended,) it may be in the power of a wicked minister to inflict on the most innocent persons such a punishment as comes little short of death, and which often occasions it. He may clap them up in a prison, keep them there for many months together, and give orders in what manner they shall be treated. Is therefore this Act, upon which every Englishman's liberty depends, only to stand in our Statute-Books, while there is no tolerable pretence, to take away mens liberties? And is it to be immediately suspended in those junctures, when innocent, but unhappy men want most that protection which this act seems particularly designed to afford them?

It must, I believe, be admitted, that what a free people, under Kingly Government, have chiefly to guard against, is, lest wicked Ministers should abuse that power they are entrusted with. A wicked Minister has an interest of his own entirely distinct from the interests of both the Prince and People; and is very little concerned, though his master is reputed cruel, bloody, or rapacious, and though his fellow-subjects are treated like slaves.

Let us reflect a little upon what has actually been done at a time, when the Habeas Corpus Act was suspended: within the memory of man, a Physician has been taken from his practice, which was computed to be worth him six hundred pounds per annum, and made a close prisoner, though the lives of a great number of persons of merit and distinction were under his care. To justify this proceeding, I have heard, that a certain modest person took upon him to affirm, in a certain assembly, that the Doctor was concerned in the blackeſt Part of a certain plot. By those words, it was generally understood, that the physician had undertaken to poison the King who was then reigning. To convince the world, how false and scandalous this insinuation was, the very daughter of that King, soon after committed her own sacred life, and the lives of her Royal Progeny, to the care of this very Physician; who after a long confinement was released out of prison, without being convicted of any crime. It ought not, indeed, to be forgot, that a few days before he was taken up, he had made a very sharp and eloquent speech in the House of Commons, of which he was a member, against the First Minister.

I proceed to say something of the treatment several persons have met with, as soon as they have been called State Criminals.

Whoever looks into those volumes, entitled State Trials, will find an account of the most infamous and inhuman murders, all committed under the formal and specious mask of Public Justice. Experience has shown us, that judges and juries have been too ready to do what they were sure would please a wicked Minister, and how difficult it is, for the most innocent man to escape, when he is called a State Criminal, and brought to his trial with the weight and influence of a Court against him.

There is one piece of ceremony, which I have often wondered at in a State Trial: when an innocent man is acquitted of the crimes which were falsely laid to his charge, it is expected, he should kneel down, and return the court public thanks for the great favour he has received. I believe it has frequently happened, that many an innocent person has been utterly ruined, by being flung into a prison, and obliged to defray the expenses of a trial, and to defend his life against the powerful attempts made to deprive him of it. In this case, the mighty favour conferred upon him when he is acquitted, seems to be little more than a gracious permission for him to starve in any part of Great Britain. I know I ought to think myself wrong, rather than to suspect that the laws or customs of my country can be so: I shall not therefore presume to affirm, that, the above mentioned, ceremony is utterly inconsistent with freedom or liberty; I shall only say, that how to reconcile them, is infinitely above my poor capacity. I beg leave to add, that our excellent Queen Elizabeth seemed to think there was something more due to an innocent man, who had been wrongly imprisoned, than barely to release him. We have seen, in the first pages of these memoirs, that she not only ordered Mr. Boyle. Afterwards Earl of Cork, to be set at liberty, but ordered that he should be fully recompensed, out of her own royal treasure, for all the damages he had sustained by his confinement. I hope, my readers will not think this short digression altogether impertinent. I return to the late Earl of Orrery.

We are obliged, in common justice, to believe that he was innocent of any crime against the state, since nothing could be proved upon him; though there seems to have been no pains omitted to search for evidences. To say he was capable of entering into any measures with such a creature as Layer, or of acting upon what is called Layer's Plan, is, in my humble opinion, to affirm in other words, that his Lordship was as much a madman, as the famous Knight Errant of La Mancha.

As to Layer himself, I believe, all who read his confession before the Council, and the paper which is in print, and called his *Scheme or Plan for an Insurrection*, will readily allow, that he was thoroughly qualified either for Bedlam or Tyburn. I am not so sure that all men will agree, to which of those places he ought to have been sent. There is one particular which no body can help observing who reads the account of the execution of this unhappy man: the poor creature had, it seems, taken more than ordinary care, that a paper, of which he left two copies, with two different persons should be published after his death. This paper has, by some means or other, been stifled, and never yet appeared: if it had we might, have been let into the true reasons why he was so often reprieved after he was condemned, and why he was at last executed.

Among all the hardships which an innocent man suffers, when a First Minister thinks fit to suspect him for a plotter, there is none greater, than that all papers relating to his private affairs, and such letters as he has received from his most intimate friends, should be seized upon, and perhaps, exposed to the inspection of his greatest enemies. I believe there is no man who has not some papers by him, which, though they contain no plot, he would be loath to have perused by other people. I must own I should think, that in a nation where we talk so much about liberty and property, nothing but the utmost necessity, and the plainest proofs, should be sufficient to authorize one man to seize upon the private papers of another, I could, perhaps, give particular instances where this power of seizing papers (which I am afraid, has sometimes been most arbitrarily assumed) has been most scandalously abused.

The Lord Orrery had been six months at liberty before he heard any news of all the papers that had been taken from him. At last, his secretary, without his Lordship's knowledge, meeting a certain gentleman in St. James's-Park, asked him, what was the reason his master's papers were not returned to him? A few days after, a messenger from the secretaries office, brought a large sack of papers, sealed up, to the Lord Orrery's house, and offered to leave it there, provided his Lordship would give him a receipt for all the papers which had been taken from him. His papers were neither marked, nor any inventory taken of them, when they were carried off: he therefore did not think proper to comply with this extraordinary demand of a receipt. The fellow was told, that he might, if he pleased, carry back his sack: he thought fit, however, to leave it sealed up; and though the Lord Orrery, had a great many papers and letters taken from him, which concerned his private affairs, and were necessary for the regulating of them, yet for certain reasons, not difficult to be guessed at, he would never open this sack to the day of his death. It came (sealed up, as the messenger had left it,) into the hands of the present Earl of Orrery.

The late Lord Orrery, having obtained his freedom, attended constantly in his place in the House of Peers, as he had done before. Though he despaired of being able to bring the majority of that assembly into his own way of thinking, he thought his attendance was an indispensable duty, and what his country had a right to expect from him. The Lord Clarendon seems to be of the same opinion, when speaking of such members who absented them from the long parliament, he says

"I shall not, I cannot, make any excuse for those (of whom somewhat is before spoken) who, from the beginning of

*this parliament, and in the whole progress of it, either out
of laziness or negligence, or incogitancy,[104] or weariness,
forbore to give their attendance there."*

Though the Lord Orrery, as I have already observed, never spoke himself in the House of Peers, his sentiments were often delivered by the mouths of others; and his pen frequently employed to draw up those protests, to which so many other Lords besides himself set their hands. These protests were usually printed, when the parliament rose; and if we may conclude anything from the reception they me with from the public, we shall be almost tempted to think, that the majority of the most illustrious assemblies are not altogether infallible.

Upon our present Sovereign's accession to the throne, (to whom his Lordship was well known, when his Majesty was Prince of Wales,) he went sometimes to Court, that he might show his respect to the King and Queen: he went thither but seldom, least he should be thought to pay his court to the Minister; whose measures and conduct he never approved.

He died, after a short indisposition on the 28th August 1731, in the 57th year of his age. His friends, and those about him, were not apprehensive that his life was in danger, till he lost his speech. I had myself the honour to be with him alone above two hours, on the Sunday morning before he died, and could then observe no alteration in him.

The last Lord Orrery seems to have united in himself some of the different talents and accomplishments of his illustrious ancestors. He had as much courage, and more wit and learning, than his grandfather; and like his great-uncle, had a genius both for mechanics and Medicine.

The instrument[105] which was invented by him, and bears his name, is an undeniable proof of his mechanic genius. There are so many different motions in this machine, that, I have heard his Lordship say,

---

[104] Incogitancy is an archaic word meaning thoughtfulness

[105] The "Orrery" is a device representing the sun and planets on the same plane showing their relative motions rather than their sizes and distances from each other. Invented in the period 1710-1712, Lord Orrery commissioned the creation of one by John Rowley and subsequently the device has become known by Orrery's name.

it had almost turned the head of that ingenious artificer, whom he employed to make it. There could not have been a more happy invention, to give such persons as are not deeply learned in astronomy, some notion of the solar system. I am told, that one of these machines, having been presented to the Emperor of China, has been highly liked and approved of by that great prince, and his mandarins: nor am I at all surprised, that the Orrery should meet with such a reception at the most polite and splendid court in the Universe, and where learning and arts, are prized, and encouraged to that degree, which I have shown in my Letter to the King of Sparta.

The Lord Orrery, had so strong a genius for Physic or Medicine, that he bought and read whatever was published on that subject; employed several persons to send him an account of drugs and herbs in foreign countries; and prescribed, with success, to many of his friends, upon several occasions. I have seen a great number of bills, all wrote with his own hand, in the style of a regular Physician; and some diaries of T*he Progress of distempers,* after the manner of *Hippocrates.*

I have already observed that he was a pupil of the late Bishop of Rochester's; and it was scarce possible for him to have had any tutor more capable of improving those great parts heaven had bestowed upon him.

What Mr. Atterbury thought of him, will appear by the following, extract, from a letter; which I shall lay before my readers, not only because it will show them what opinion that great genius had of Mr. Boyle, but because it is likewise and evidence, what the consciousness of his own abilities forced him to think of himself, while he was yet a young man.

> "—— *My pupil, I never had a thought of parting with, till I left Oxford —— I wish I could part with him to morrow on that score; For I am perfectly wearied with this nauseous circle of small affairs, that can now neither divert, nor instruct me. I was made, I am sure, for another scene, and another sort of conversation; though it has been my hard luck, to be pinn'd down to this. I have thought, and thought again, Sir, and for some years: Now I have never been able*

to think otherwise, than that I am loosing time every
minute I stay here. The only benefit I ever propose to myself
by the place, is studying; and that I am not able to compass.
Mr Boyle, takes up half my time, and I grudge it him not;
for he's a fine gentleman: And while I am with him, I'll do
what I can to make him a man. College and University
business take up a great deal more; and I am forced to be
useful to the Dean, in a thousand particulars; so that I have
very little time
Oxford, October 24, 1690.
Sir,
Your most dutiful son,
Fr. Atterbury."

Mr. Atterbury was as good as his word: the late Earl of Orrery, who was a fine gentleman, when he was put into his hands, came out of them a man, in the best and truest signification of the word. To his tutor he probably owed a good part of that fine relish he had, for the writings of the ancients. He made these his constant study; but expressed an high contempt, for the greatest part our modern wits and authors. He confessed, indeed, that here and there, a genius was to be found, whose matter and style evidently showed that he tasted the beauties of the ancients, and formed himself upon them.

He had a great and open way of thinking of that homage and adoration which men owe to the supreme Being; but looked upon himself obliged to conform in public to the established religion of his country, and neither to say or advance any thing which might bring that religion into contempt. His behaviour in this particular, seems to be agreeable to what has been the conduct of the greatest and wisest men in all ages: it is very remarkable, that the golden verses of Pythagoras, begin with this precept,

Aθανatᵽs πℨϖta θℇᵽs, voµϖ ϖs diaχɛtai, Tiµã.[106]

---

[106] "The immortal God Piola, reverence as by law arranged"

Where the word νομω , if I am not mistaken, plainly shows that the author of these verses meant the religion established by LAW.

As a statesman, he aimed at nothing but what he sincerely believed was for the real advantage and benefit of his country: he was as great a lover of liberty, as far from any slavish principles, or from suffering bad Ministers to screen themselves with any pretended prerogatives of the crown while they encroached upon the freedom of the people, as any one man in all England. He was delighted with the company of two sorts of persons; either with such as were really geniuses of the first rank, who had fine understandings, strong judgments, and true tastes; or with such as had a few foibles, and an eye of ridicule in them, which served to make him laugh. He would railly these in so agreeable, and yet in so tender a manner, that though it diverted himself and others, was never offensive to the person he raillied. It cannot be expected, that I should name such of his acquaintances as were in the last class: some of those who stood foremost in the first class, were the present Earl of Anglesey, Sir Thomas Hanmer,[107] and the Lady Sandwich.[108] This Lady is both an honour and disgrace to her native country: she resides at Paris, highly valued and admired by the greatest men, and finest wits in France: but it is a melancholy reflection, that we have either nothing in England valuable enough to make her prefer her own country to another, or that we will not suffer such a person to reside quietly among us.

In whatever company the late Lord Orrery appeared, his fine sense, his wit, and his learning were so well known, that they gave him a sort of natural ascendant: every man paid a deference to his judgment, and

[107] **Hanmer, Sir Thomas (1677-1746):** He was speaker of the House of Commons and was the only surviving son of William Hanmer. He was born at Bettisfield Park, in the parish of Hanmer, Flintshire, the residence of his grandfather, Sir Thomas Hanmer, on 24 Sept. 1677. Hanmer was educated at Westminster School, and afterwards at Christ Church, Oxford. He produced a famous edition of the works of Shakespeare and died on 7th May 1746.

[108] **Montagu, Lady Mary Wortley Lady Sandwich (1689-1762):** From her early years she was a precocious reader and was encouraged by an uncle, William Feilding (Earl of Denbigh), and by Bishop Burnet. Despite reservation from her family she married Edward Wortley Montagu, privately by special license, dated 12th August 1712. She published various tracts and became well known to all the wits, and among others to Pope, who professed especial admiration for her. Her husband was posted to Turkey and while there she noticed the practice of inoculation for small-pox and was largely responsible for the introduction of the practice in England. For many years after her return to England she was a leader in London society. A major quarrel and literary debate with Pope led to questions about her reputation and suggestion of both dishonesty and a possible affair. This led to the spoiling of her position in society and relationship with her husband, subsequently leading to her emigration to France in 1739. Her letters to her husband imply that they still remained on friendly terms, and while she suggested that she expected him to follow her they did not meet again. She spent the rest of her life in travel around Europe and died on 21st August 1762.

seemed afraid either to do a rude thing, or to say a silly one before him: whenever he came into a public coffeehouse, or a mixed company, a certain politeness was immediately observed in the conversation, which was visibly owing to his presence. In mixed company he appeared a man of sense and a fine gentleman; but none knew the real beauties of his mind, besides those few friends with whom he has conversed freely and alone. The great Mr. Addison used to call a man's talking to a friend, in whom he had an entire confidence, thinking aloud. Whoever has had the pleasure to hear the late Lord Orrery think aloud, could not but observe in him a wonderful strength of judgment, an exact knowledge of the world, and, a most uncommon penetration into the real designs and characters of men. He was man of honour in the strictest and highest sense of the expression; and true to every engagement and friendship into which he once entered: his character was so well known and established in this point, that there are some worthy persons living, who, though they had no reserve for him, will, I believe, never place the same confidence in any other man, He was never charged through the whole course of his life with a mean action, or with violating the laws of friendship. He did not always meet with the same treatment from those who had acted in concert with him, and promised in the most solemn manner, that no views of interest should tempt them to desert him. If ever he was obliged to talk of these persons, (which he did not willingly do,) he always spoke of them rather with a generous compassion for their weakness, than with any resentment of the usage he had received from them. While he remained fixed in his own principles, he found himself at different times courted and applied to by most of those great Ministers who once acted in direct opposition to him. The late Earl of Halifax acquainted him with his design of laying down his post of First Lord of the Treasury, and in what manner he intended to act afterwards. The late Lord Sunderland[109] earnestly courted his friendship; and, but a few days before he died, made him a visit, and had a long conference with him upon some points of the utmost importance. He had a natural

---

[109] **Spencer, Robert, 2nd Earl of Sunderland (1640-1702):** He was the only son and heir of Henry Spencer, matriculating from Magdalen College, Oxford, in 1635, and receiving his M.A. in 1636. On 19th December 1636 Spencer succeeded as third baron. He ensured the continuance of the family following the assent of William. He did not long survive William being taken ill at Althorp and dying on 28th September 1702

love and esteem for men of parts and learning. In his expenses, he was extremely regular; and was neither profuse or avaricious. No man was more beloved in his own family, or better maintained the figure of an English nobleman. He kept a most elegant table, pretty much in the French way, and was never better pleased, than when he saw it filled with his friends. His manner of entertaining them was perfectly easy and polite. No man living was of a more easy access to those he valued: to such, he was always at home, and never denied; at the same time, he did not think himself obliged to carry the point of ceremony so far, as to lose much of his time with people whom he despised, or did not care for; and he desired to be excused from admitting the visits of some men of the first quality. He was usually up by six in the morning. I have myself more than once walked over the Park with him from his own house, and seen him on horseback by seven, an hour, at which, I am afraid, most of our English nobility are commonly in a state of as much inaction, as if they were really dead. His dress was always neat, and sometimes gay; but he had something so naturally genteel in the make of his person, and his whole behaviour, that no dress, however mean, could hinder him from looking like a man of quality. He was of a middle size, and so very slender, and had such a gait, that a stranger to him, who had walked behind him, would have taken him, the very year he died, for a young fellow of five and twenty. He was short-sighted; and two or three other celebrated wits happening to have the same blemish, the fops of the town, who had an ambition to be thought wits, all of them affected to appear short sighted. I will not venture to affirm that no man in England is a finer gentleman, or a better scholar, than the late Earl of Orrery; yet I believe I may truly assert, that he has not left a man behind him, in whose single person we can find more learning, and more politeness united together.

Having considered his virtues and accomplishments, I should not act the part of an impartial historian, if I said noting of those faults which have been laid to his charge. He is accused by some people with having taken too great liberties with respect to women: at the same time there are many who deny this to be a fault; and three parts in four of the Christian World affirm, that it is at most but a venial one. Without going so far, I shall only say, that if it be a fault, some of the greatest men in all ages have been guilty of it; for which, perhaps, a natural reason might be given. Perhaps those very animal spirits, which by their fineness and quantity, are the immediate cause of wisdom, wit, and courage, do naturally and strongly incline those men, in whom they reside, to the commission of this fault.

His Lordship has been likewise blamed for too easily confiding in men, who did not deserve to be trusted. Perhaps the generosity of his temper, and too good an opinion of mankind, might lead him into this error, when he was a young man; but I have reasons to say, that experience, and a thorough knowledge of the world, had taught him another sort of conduct for many years before he died.

Lastly, he has been blamed for being too negligent in the care of his private fortune. I believe it is true, that a little before his death, he discovered, that a person entrusted with his affairs in Ireland, (where he had a noble estate,) had not returned him one half of the yearly income for which several of his estates were actually set, and that he had determined to call this person to an account. He was nevertheless so good a manager of that yearly income he received, that though, as I have before observed, he lived as an English nobleman ought to live, he left the present Earl of Orrery, not only a clear estate, but a considerable sum in ready money, and as much plate as was valued at £6000.

By his will, he bequeathed several generous and good-natured legacies, to such persons as he loved and esteemed: but there is one article in his will, which, as it has made some noise in the world, deserves to be explained: What I shall say upon this head, is, to my own certain knowledge, matter of fact. The late Lord Orrery, has bequeathed to Christ-Church College in Oxford, of which he was formerly a member, all his noble library, save only the Journals of the House of Lords, and such books as relate to the English history and constitution which are left to the present Earl his son; who is likewise allowed the term of two years, to separate these books from the other books. The world has been not a little surprised, to find that the late Earl of Orrery, should leave the bulk of that library, he had collected with so much pains and expense, from such a son; from a son, whom all who have the happiness to know him, do very well know, is not only learned, but a real lover of learning and men of letters. In order to explain this mystery, it is proper the public should be informed, that the late Lord Orrery's will, was made about four years since, at a time, when there was an unhappy coldness between him and his son. This coldness was occasioned by a family difference between the late Earl of Orrery and the present Earl of Orkney,[110] soon after the son of the first, had married the daughter of the latter. Perhaps neither of these two noble Lords, were wholly in the wrong: there are some things of so tender a nature, that though they are reasonable enough in themselves, they may become unreasonable, by being insisted upon, at an improper time, or in an improper manner. The present Earl of Orrery, upon this unfortunate misunderstanding, between his own father and his father-in-law, found himself in a very unhappy situation: it was scarce possible for him not to disoblige either a wife whom he tenderly loved, and who well deserves all his love, or a father, whom, he both loved and respected in the highest degree. He resolved, however, if possible to do neither; fully persuaded, that his father's excellent understanding would soon oblige him to reflect upon the unhappy circumstances his son was in. He was not mistaken: a coldness could not long subsist between such a father and such a son; they soon ran into each others arms: the little coldness there had been between them, served but to endear them to each other the more, and make them resolve, that no future accident should lessen their affections. Whoever saw them together, and they were seldom asunder when in town, would not have taken them for a father and son, but for two men of quality, between whom there was a most strict and intimate friendship. The late Lord Orrery now plainly saw all the value of his son, and was so much pleased with him, that he could hardly be easy without him. He resolved before he went to Paris, for which place he was to have set out, but a few days after he died, to have cancelled that will, which he had made in a passion, and to have left his library to his son, who he was fully convinced deserved it as well, and was as likely to make a proper use of it, as any young

---

[110] **Hamilton, Lord George, Earl of Orkney (1666-1737):** He was fifth son of William, Earl of Selkirk (eldest son of William, marquis of Douglas). He was born at Hamilton Palace, Lanark, and baptised there 9th February 1666. He died at his residence in Albemarle Street, London, on 29th January 1737.

nobleman in Great Britain: to this purpose, he had actually sent to that gentleman to come to him, who had made his will about four years before.

He was, however, prevented from altering that Will, by his death, which happened in that sudden and unexpected manner, we have already taken notice of.

The present Earl of Orrery's friends, have often heard him say, that though he cannot help wishing his father had left him his library, and would gladly purchase it at any rate, yet, since he is deprived of so valuable a treasure himself, he is pleased to think it will go to Christ-Church, the college to which he owes his own academical education: and I have reasons to believe, that his Lordship intends to send the library of his deceased father to Christ-Church, in such a manner, as will fully convince that learned society, how sincere a respect he has for them.

The legacy left them by the late Lord Orrery, is indeed a noble one: I can speak of his library with the more certainty, as I had a constant access to it, and a key left for me, whenever he went out of town.

He had three large rooms filled with books. In the first room he ranged his French and Italian books, and in the second his English; the third and innermost room, which was much the largest, was filled with Greek and Latin authors. He had likewise, a fine collection of mathematical instruments.

The most valuable library of any nobleman's in England, is doubtless, the Lord Sunderland's. The late Earl of Sunderland spared no cost to collect it, gave any money for a valuable or scarce edition of a book, and has frequently nine or ten several editions of the same book. The late Orrery collected his library after another manner, and has generally speaking, but one good edition, seldom or never more than two editions of the same book; so that though there were not so great a number of volumes in his library, as in the Lord Sunderland's, I believe, he had as many different books.

The present Earl of Orrery, was so truly afflicted with the death of his father, that it flung him into a fit of sickness, which had like to have cost him his life; and obliged him to go to the Bath. While he was at this place, one of his friends sent him a letter of condolence, upon the death of his father, in which were the following verses.

> *"'Tis said for every common Grief,*
> *The Muses can afford relief;*
> *And surely on that heavenly Train,*
> *A Boyle can never call in vain.*
> *Then strait invoke the sacred nine,*
> *Nor impions slight their gifts divine;*
> *Dispel those clouds that damp your fire;*
> *Shew Bath like Tunbridge,*[111] *can inspire"*

To these verses, his Lordship returns the following answer

> *"Nor Bath, not Tunbridge, can my lays*
> *inspire,*
> *Nor radiant beauty make me strike the lire;*
> *Far from the busy crowd, I sit forlorn,*
> *And sigh in secret, and in silence mourn;*
> *Nor can my anguish ever find an end,*
> *I weep a Father, but I've lost a friend."*

I have ventured to oblige my readers with these lines, since I find they are already got into several hands; insomuch that I myself had them from a person, who is no way related to the Lord Orrery.

I shall conclude these memoirs of the family of the Boyles, with the same observation with which I began them, namely, that there have been always some of its descendants more remarkable and conspicuous for their personal merit, and undoubted abilities, than for their birth, their titles, or estates.

The present Earls of Burlington and Orrery, the two eldest branches of this illustrious family, are remarkable for their great natural parts, their fine taste, and their love of letters, and men of learning. I am sorry, I am able to add that these virtues and accomplishments, do but

---

111 The present Earl of Orrery, had written some humorous verses, when he was at Tunbridge, the year before his father died.

too much distinguish them, from the body of the British nobility.

The Lord Viscount Shannon, who is the youngest branch of this family, is at present General of all his Majesty's forces in Ireland. As this noble Lord's education has been chiefly in a Camp, I have never heard, that he has a more than ordinary share of learning; but all who know him, know, that he is brave and generous; that he has an openness and frankness in his conversation, which are highly engaging; and, in a word, that he has the necessary qualifications to make himself beloved in an English army.

FINIS

Appendix,
Relating to the Honourable Robert Boyle, Esq.

 t is matter of the greatest surprise, how any gentleman could pretend to write an account of the family of Boyle, and say so little of the noblest benefactor that ever sprung from it. In justice to the memory of the Honourable Robert Boyle, Esq; and to the public, I have collected some memorials of his unparalleled munificence and private character, from the records of one who was well known to him, viz.

On the 7th Day of January 1692, a sermon was preached at the Parish Church of St. Martin in the Fields, at the funeral of this illustrious personage, by the Right Reverend Father in God, Gilbert Burnet, D.D. Lord Bishop of Sarum.

In this most excellent discourse, the orator seems to have exhausted all that could be inferred from his text,[112] in the most eloquent manner, and yet, from his own knowledge, makes the following declaration, viz.

I know, says Bishop Burnet, I ought here to raise my style, and to triumph upon the honour that belongs to religion and virtue, and that appeared so eminently in a life, which may be considered as a pattern of living; and a pattern so perfect, that it will, perhaps seem a little too far out of sight, too much above the hopes and by consequence, above

---

[112] God giveth to a man that is good in his sight, wisdom knowledge and joy. Eccles. II 26

the endeavours of any that might pretend to draw after such an original; which must ever be reckoned amongst the masterpieces, even of that great hand that made it. I might here challenge the whole tribe of Libertines, to come and view the usefulness, as well as the excellence of the Christian Religion, in a life that was entirely dedicated to it, and see what they can object. I ought to call on all that were so happy, as to know him well, to observe his temper and course of life, and charge them to sum up, and lay together, the many great and good things that they saw in him; and from thence to remember always to how vast a sublimity the Christian Religion can raise a mind, that does both thoroughly believe it, and is entirely governed by it. I might here also call up the multitudes, the vast multitudes, of those who have been made both the wiser and the easier, the better and the happier, by his means; but that I might do all this with the more advantage, I ought to bring it all, at once, into my memory, the many happy hours that, in a course of nine and twenty years conversation, have fallen to my own share, which were very frequent and free for about half that time; that have so often both humbled and raised me, by feeling how exalted he was, and in that feeling more sensibly my own nothing and depression, and which have always edified and never once, nor in any one thing, been uneasy to me. When I remember how much I saw in him, and learned, or, at least might have learned from him; when I reflect on the gravity of his very appearance, the elevation of his thoughts and discourses, the modesty of his temper, and the humility of his whole deportment, which might have served to have forced the best thoughts, even upon the worst minds; when I say, I bring all this together into my mind, as I form upon it too bright an idea to be easily received by such as did not know him, so I am very sensible that I cannot raise it, equal to the thoughts of such as did. I am resolved to use great reserves; and to manage a tenderness, which, how much soever it may melt me, shall not carry me beyond the strictest measures, and I will study to keep as much within bounds, as he lived beyond them.

I will say nothing of the stem from which he sprang; that watered garden, watered with the blessings and dew of heaven. As well as fed with the best portions of this life, that has produced so many noble plants, and has stocked the most families of these kingdoms of many in our age; which has so signally felt the effects of their humble and Christian motto, *God's Providence is my Inheritance*. He was the only brother of five, that had none of these titles that found high in the world; but he procured one to himself, which, without derogating from the dignity of Kings, must be acknowledged to be beyond their prerogative. He had a great and noble fortune; but it was chiefly so to him, because he had a great and noble mind to employ it to the best uses. He began early to show both a probity, and a capacity, that promised great things; and he passed through the youthful parts of life, with so little of the youth in him, that, in his travels, while he was very young, and wholly the master of himself, he seemed to be out of the reach of the disorders of that age, and those countries through which he passed. He had a modesty and a purity laid so deep in his nature, that those who knew him the earliest, have often told me, that even then, nature seemed entirely sanctified in him. His piety received a vast increase as he often owned to me, from his acquaintance with the great primate of Ireland, the never enough admired Ussher; who, as he was very particularly the friend of the whole family so seeing such seed and beginnings in him, studied to cultivate them with due care. He sat him chiefly to the study of the scriptures, in their original languages, which he followed in a course of many years, with so great exactness, he could have quoted all remarkable passages very readily in Hebrew; and he read the New Testament so diligently in Greek, that there never occurred to me an occasion to mention any one passage of it, that he did not readily repeat in that language. The use of this he continued to the last, for he could read it with other men's eyes; but the weakness of his sight forced him to disuse the other, since he had none about him that could read it to him. He had studied the scriptures to so good purpose, and with so critical a strictness, that few men, whose profession oblige them chiefly to that sort of learning, have gone beyond him in it: and he had so great a regard to that Sacred Book, that if any one, in discourse, had dropped anything that gave him a cleared view of any passage in it, he received it with great pleasure, he examined it accurately, and if it was not uneasy to him that offered it, he desired to have it in writing. He had the profoundest veneration for the great God of Heaven and Earth, that I have ever observed in any person. The very name of God was never mentioned by him without a pause, and a visible stop in his discourse, in which, one that knew him most particularly above twenty years, has told me, that he was so exact, that he does not remember to have observed him once to fail in it.

He was most constant and serious in his secret addresses to God; and indeed, it appeared to those who conversed most with him in his Enquiries into nature, that his main design in that, on which, as he had his own eye most constantly, so he took care to put others often in mind of it, was to raise, in himself, and others, vaster thoughts of the greatness and glory, and of the wisdom and goodness of God. This was so deep in his thoughts, that he concludes the article of his will, which relates to that illustrious body the Royal Society, in these words, wishing them also a happy success in their laudable attempts, to discover the true nature of the works of God, and praying, that they, and all other searchers into Physical Truths, may cordially refer their attainments to the glory of the great author of nature, and to the comfort of mankind. As he was a very devout worshipper of God, so he was a no less devout Christian. He had professed himself with such an amiable view of that holy religion, separated from either superstitious practices, or the sourness of parties, that, as he was fully persuaded of the truth of it, and, indeed, wholly possessed with it, so he rejoiced in every discovery that nature furnished him with, to illustrate it, or to take off the objections against any part of it. He always considered it as a system of truths, which ought to purify the hearts and govern the lives of those who profess it; he loved no practice that seemed to lessen that, nor any nicety that occasioned divisions amongst Christians. He thought pure and disinterested Christianity was so bright and glorious a thing, that he was much troubled at the disputes and divisions which had arisen about some lesser matters, while the great, and the most important, as well as the most universally acknowledged truths, were, by all sides, almost as generally neglected as they were confessed. He had therefore designed, though some accidents did, upon great considerations, divert him from settling it during his life, but not from ordering it by his will, that a liberal provision should be made for one, who should, in a very few well-digested sermons, every year, set forth the truth of the Christian Religion in general, without descending to the subdivisions among Christians, and who should be changed every third year, that so this noble study and employment might pass through many hands; by which means many might become masters of the argument. He was at the charge of the translation and impression of the New Testament into the Malayan language, which he sent over all the East-Indies. He gave a noble reward to him that translated Grotius's incomparable Book of the Truth of the Christian Religion into Arabic and was at the charge of a whole impression, which he took care to order to be scattered in all the countries where that language is understood. He was resolved to have carried on the impression of the New Testament in the Turkish language, but the company thought it became them to be the doers of it, and so suffered him only to give a large share towards it. He was at seven hundred pounds charge in the edition of the Irish bible, which he ordered to be distributed in Ireland; and he contributed liberally, both to the impression of the Welsh Bible, and of the Irish bible, for Scotland. He gave, during his life, three hundred pounds to advance the design of propagating the Christian religion in America; and as soon as he heard that the East-India Company were entertaining propositions for the like design in the East, he presently sent a hundred pounds for a beginning and an example, but intended to carry it much further, when it should be set on foot to purpose. Thus was his zeal lively and effectual in the greatest and truest concerns of religion; but he avoided to enter far into the unhappy breaches that have so long weakened; as well as distracted Christianity, any otherwise than to have a great aversion to all those opinions and practices, that seemed to him to destroy morality and charity. He had a most particular zeal against all severities and persecutions upon the account of religion. I have seldom observed him to speak with more heat and indignation, than when that came in his way. He did throughly agree with the doctrines of our Church, and conform to our worship; and he approved of the main of our constitution, but he much lamented some abuses that he thought remained still among us. He gave eminent instances of his value for the clergy; two of these I shall only mention. When he understood what a share he had in impropriations, he ordered very large gifts to be made to the Incumbents in those Parishes, and to the widows of such as had died before he had resolved on this charity. The sums that, as I have been informed, by one that was concerned in two distributions that were made, amounted upon those two occasions, to near six hundred pounds; and another very liberal one is also ordered by his Will, but in an indefinite sum, I suppose, by reason of the present condition of estates in Ireland; so plentifully did he supply those who served at the altar, out of that which was once devoted to it, though it be now converted to a temporal estate. Another instance of his sense of the sacred functions which went much deeper. Soon after the restoration, in the year sixty, the great Minister[113] of that time, pressed him, both by himself, and by another, who was then likewise in a high post, to enter into Orders: He did it not merely out of a respect to him and his family, but chiefly out of his regard to the Church, that he thought would receive a great strengthening, as well as a powerful example, from one, who, if he once entered into Holy Orders, would be quickly at the top. This, he told me, made some impressions on him. His mind was, even then, at three and thirty, so entirely disengaged from all the projects and concerns of this world, that, as the prospect of dignity in the church, could not move him much, so the probabilities of his doing good in it, was much the stronger motive. Two things determined him against it; one was, that his having no other interests, with relation to religion, besides those of saving his own soul, gave him, as he thought, a more unsuspected authority in writing, or acting on that side: he knew the profane crew fortified themselves against all that was said, by men of our profession, with this, that it was their trade, and that they were paid for it; he hoped therefore, that he might have the more influence, the less he shared in the patrimony of the Church: but his main reason was, that he had so high a sense of the obligations of the pastoral care; and of such as watch over those souls, which Christ purchased with his own blood, and for which they must give an account, at the last and

---

[113] Earl of Shaftsbury.

great day, that he durst not undertake it, especially, not having felt, within himself, an inward motion to it by the Holy Ghost; and the first question that is put to those who come to be initiated into the service of the Church, relating to that motion, he who had not felt it, thought he durst not make the step, lest, otherwise, he should have lied to the Holy Ghost; so solemnly and seriously did he judge of sacred matters. He was constant to the Church, and went to no separated assemblies, how charitably soever he might think of their persons, and how plentifully soever he might have relieved their necessities. He loved no narrow thoughts, nor low, or superstitious opinions in religion, and therefore, as he did not shut himself up within a party, so neither did he shut any party out from him. He had brought his mind to such a freedom, that he was not apt to be imposed on; and his modesty was such, that he did not dictate to others; but proposed his own sense, with a due and decent distrust, and was ever very ready to hearken to what was suggested to him by others. When he differed from any, he expressed himself in so humble, and so obliging a way, that he never treated things, or persons, with neglect; and I never heard that he offended any one person in his whole life, by any part of his deportment; for if at any time he saw cause to speak roundly to any, it was never in passion, or with any reproachful or indecent expressions. And as he was careful to give those, who conversed with him, no cause or colour for displeasure, so he was yet more careful of those who were absent, never to speak ill of any, in which he was the exactest man I ever knew. If the discourse turned to be hard on any he was presently silent; and if the subject was too long dwelt on, he would, at last, interpose, and, between reproof and raillery, divert it.

He was exactly civil, rather to ceremony; and though he felt his easiness of access, and the desires of many, all strangers in particular, to be much with him, made great wastes on his time, yet, as he was severe in that, not to be denied, when he was at home, so, he said, he knew the heart of a stranger, and how much eased his own had been, while travelling, if admitted to the conversation of those he desired to see; therefore he thought his obligation to strangers was more than bare civility; it was a piece of religious charity to him.

He had for almost forty years, laboured under such a feebleness of body, and such lowness of strength and spirits, that it will appear a surprising thing to imagine, how it was possible for him to read, to mediate, to try experiments, and to write as he did. He bore all his infirmities, and some sharp pains, with the decency and submission that became a Christian and a Philosopher. He had about him all that unaffected neglect of pomp in clothes, lodging, furniture and equipage, which agreed with his grave and serious course in life. He was advised to a very ungrateful simplicity of diet; which, by all appearance, was that which preserved him so long beyond all men's expectations; this he observed served so strictly, that, in a course of above thirty years, he neither eat nor drank to gratify the varieties of appetite, but merely to support nature; and was so regular in it, that he never once transgressed the rule, measure, and kind, that was prescribed him. He had a feebleness in his sight, his eyes were so well used by him, that it would be easily imagined he was very tender of them, and very apprehensive of such distempers as might affect them. He did also imagine, that if sickness obliged him to lie long in bed, it might raise the pains of the stone in him to a degree that was above his weak strength to bear; so that he feared that his last minutes might be too hard for him; and this was the root of all the caution and apprehension that he was observed to live in: but as to life itself, he had the just indifference to it, and the weariness of it, that became so true a Christian: I mention these the rather, that I may have occasion to show the goodness of God to him, in the two things that he feared for his sight began not to grow dim above four hours before he died; and when death came upon him, he had not been above three hours a bed, before it made an end of him, with so little uneasiness, that it was plain the light went out, merely for want of oil to maintain the flame.

But I have looked so early to the conclusion of his life, yet before I can come at it, I find there is still much in my way. His charity to those that were in want, and his bounty to all learned men, that were put to wrestle with difficulties, were so very extraordinary, and so many did partake of them, that I may spend a little time on this article. Great sums went easily from him, without the partialities of sect, country, or relations; for he considered himself as a part of the human nature, and as a debtor to the whole race of men. He took care to do this so secretly, that even those who knew all his other concerns, could never find out what he did that way; and, indeed, he was so strict to our Saviour's Precept; that, except the persons themselves, or some one whom he trusted to convey it to them, nobody ever knew how that great share of his estate, which went away invisibly, was distributed; even he himself kept no account of it, for that, he thought, might fall into other hands. I speak upon full knowledge on this article, because I had the honour to be often made use of by him in it. If those that have fled hither from the persecutions of France, or from the calamities of Ireland, feel a sensible sinking of their secret supplies, with which they were often furnished, without knowing from whence they came, they will conclude, that they have lost, not only a purse, but an estate that went so very liberally among them, that I have reason to say, that, for some years, his charity went beyond a thousand pounds a year.

Here I thought to have gone to another head, but the relation he had, both in nature and grace, in living and dying, in friendship, and a likeness of soul to another person, forces me, for a little while, to change my subject. I have been restrained from it by some of her relations, but since I was not so by herself, I must give a little vent to nature and to friendship; to a long acquaintance and a vast esteem. His sister and he were pleasant in their lives, and in their death they were not divided; for as he lived with her above forty years, so he did not out live her above a week. Both died from the same cause, nature being quite spent in both. She lived the longest on the publickest scene; she made the greatest figure in all the revolutions of these kingdoms for above fifty years, of any woman of our age: she employed it all for doing good to others, in which she laid out her time, her interest, and her estate, with the greatest zeal, and the most success, that I have ever known. She was indefatigable, as well as dexterous, in it; and as her great understanding, and the vast esteem she was in, made all persons, in their several turns of greatness, desire and value her friendship; so she gave herself a clear title to employ her interest with them for the service of others, by this, that she never made any use of it to any end or design of her own: she was contented with what she had; and, though she was twice stripped of it, she never moved on her own account, but was the general intercessor for all persons of merit, or in want; this had in her the better grace, and was both more Christian and more effectual, because it was not limited within any narrow compass of parties or relations. When any party was down, she had credit and zeal enough to serve them; and she employed that so effectually, that, in the next turn, she had a new stock of credit, which she laid out wholly in that labour of love, in which she spent her life; and though some particular opinions might shut her up in a divided communion, yet her soul was never of a party: she divided her charities and friendships both, her esteem, as well as her bounty, with the truest regard to merit, and her own obligations, without any difference made upon the account of opinion.

She had, with a vast reach, both the knowledge and apprehensions, an universal affability and easiness of access, a humility that descended to the meanest persons and concerns, an obliging kindness, and readiness to advise those who had no occasion for any further assistance from her; and with all these, and many more, excellent qualities, she had the deepest sense of religion, and the most constant turning of her thoughts and discourses that way, that has been, perhaps in our age. Such a sister became such a brother; and it was but suitable to both their characters, that they should have improved the relation, under which they were born, to the most exalted and endearing one of friend. At any time a nation may very ill spare one such; but for both to go at once, and at such a time, is too melancholy a thought; and notwithstanding the decline of their age, and the waste of their strength, yet it has too much of cloud in it, to bear being long dwelt on.

Thus are seen in a very few hints, the several sorts, and instances of goodness that appeared in this life, which has now its period; that which gives value and lustre to them all was, that whatever he might be in the sight of men, how pure and spotless soever, those, who knew him the best, have reason to conclude, that he was much more so in the sight of God, for they had often occasions to discover new instances of goodness in him; and no secret ill inclinations did at any time show themselves. He affected nothing that was solemn or supercilious: he used no methods to make multitudes run after him, or depend upon him. It never appeared that there was any thing hid, under all this appearance of goodness, that was not truly so. He hid both his piety and charity all he could. He lived in the due methods of civility, and would never assume the authority which all the world was ready to pay him. He spoke of the Government, even in times which he disliked, and upon occasions which he spared not to condemn, with an exactness of respect. He allowed himself a great deal of decent cheerfulness, so that he had nothing of the moroseness, to which philosophers think they have some right; nor of the affections, which men of an extraordinary pitch of devotion go into, sometimes, without being well aware of them. He was, in a word, plainly and sincerely in the sight of God, as well as in the view of men, a good man, even one of a thousand.

That, which comes next to be considered is the share, that this good man had in those gifts of God, wisdom, knowledge and joy. If I should speak of these, with the copiousness which the subject affords, I should be too prolix; I will therefore name things which may only be enlarged on more fully another way. He had too unblemished a candour to be capable of those arts and practices, that a false and deceitful world may call wisdom. He could neither lie nor equivocate; but he could well be silent, and by practicing that much, he covered himself upon many uneasy occasions. He made true judgments of men and things. His advices and opinions were solid and sound; and if caution and modesty gave too strong a bias, his invention was fruitful to suggest good expedients. He had great notions of what human nature might be brought to; but since he saw mankind was not capable of them, he withdrew himself early from affairs and courts, notwithstanding the distinction with which he was always treated by two succeeding Princes.[114] But he had the principles of an Englishman, as well of a Protestant, too deep in him to be corrupted or cheated out of them; and, in these he studied to fortify all that conversed much with him. He had a very particular sagacity in observing what men were fit for;

---

114 King Charles and King James II

and had so vast a scheme of different performances, that he could soon furnish every man with work that had leisure and capacity for it, and, as soon as he saw him engaged in it then a handsome present was made to enable him to go on with it.

His knowledge was of so vast an extent, that if it were not for the variety of vouchers in their several sorts, I should be afraid to say all I know. He carried the study of the Hebrew very far into the Rabbinical writings, and the other Oriental languages. He had read so much of the Fathers, that he had formed out of it a clear judgment of all the eminent ones. He had read a vast deal on the scriptures and had gone very nicely through the whole controversies of religion; and was a true master in the whole body of Divinity. He run the whole compass of the mathematical sciences; and though he did not set himself to spring new game, yet he knew even the abstrusest parts of geometry, geography, in the several parts of it that related to navigation, or travelling; history, and books of travels, were his diversions. He went very nicely through all the parts of Physick, only the tenderness of his nature made him less able to endure the exactness of anatomical dissections, especially of living animals, though he knew these to be the most instructing: but for the history of nature, ancient and modern, of the productions of all countries, of the virtues and improvements of plants, or ores and minerals, and all the varieties that are in them in different climates: he was, by much, by very much, the readiest and the perfectest I ever knew, in the greatest compass, and with the truest exactness. This put him in the way of making all that vast variety of experiments, beyond any man, as far as we know, that ever lived. And in these, as he made a great progress in new discoveries, so he used so nice a strictness, and delivered them with so scrupulous a truth, that all, who have examined them, have found how safely the world may depend upon them. But his peculiar and favourite study was Chemistry; in which he engaged with none of those ravenous and ambitious designs that draw many into them. His design was only to find out nature, to see into what principles things might be resolved, and of what they were compounded, and to prepare good medicaments for the bodies of men. He spent neither his time nor fortune upon the vain pursuits of high promises and pretensions. He always kept himself within the compass that his estate might well bear; and as he made Chemistry much better for his dealing in it, so he never made himself either the worse or the poorer for it. It was a charity to others, as well as an entertainment to himself; for the produce of it was distributed by his sister, and others, into whose hands he put it. I will not here amuse you with a list of his astonishing knowledge, or of his great performances this way: they are highly valued all the world over, and his name is every where mentioned with most particular characters of respect. I will conclude this article with a remark, in which I appeal to all competent judges, that few men (if any) have been known so exact in all the parts of it as he was.

As for joy, he had, indeed, nothing of frolic and levity in him, he had no relish, for the idle and extravagant madness of the men of pleasure; he did not waste his time, nor dissipate his spirits into foolish mirth, but he professed his own soul in patience, full of that solid joy which his goodness, as well as his knowledge, afforded him: he who had neither designs nor passions, was capable of little trouble from any concerns of his own: he had about him all the tenderness of good nature, as well as all the softness of friendship; these gave him a large share of other men's concerns; for he had a quick sense of the miseries of mankind. He had also a feeble body, which needed to be looked to the more, because his mind went faster than that his body could keep pace with it; yet his great thoughts of God, and his contemplation of his works, were to him sources of joy, which could never be exhausted. The sense of his own integrity, and of the good he found it did, afforded him the truest of all pleasures, since they gave him the certain prospect of the fullness of joy, in the sight of which he lived so long, and in the possession of which he now lives, and shall live for ever; and this spent and exhausted body shall then put on a new form, and be made a fit dwelling for that pure and exalted mind in the final restitution.

Extracted from the Registry of the Prerogative Court of Canterbury.

In the third codicil annexed to the testament, or last will, of the Honourable Robert Boyle, Esq; late of Stalbridge, in the County of Dorset, deceased, bearing date the 28th day of July, in the year of our Lord God 1691, remaining in the Registry of this Court, amongst other things, therein is contained as follows, viz.

Whereas I have an intention to settle in my life time, the sum of fifty pounds per annum for ever, or, at least, for a considerable number of years, to be for an annual salary for some learned Divine, or preaching minister, from time to time to be elected and resident within the City of London, or Circuit of the Bills of Mortality, who shall be enjoined to perform the offices following, viz.

To preach eight sermons in the year, for proving the Christian religion, against notorious infidels, viz. atheists, thieves, pagans, Jews, and Mohammedans, not descending lower to any controversies that are among Christians themselves: These lectures to be on the first Monday of the respective months of January, February, March, April, May September, October, November, in such church as my trustees herein named shall from time to time appoint to be assisting to all companies, and encouraging of them in any undertakings for propagating the Christina religion to foreign parts; to be ready to satisfy such real scruples as any may have concerning those matters; and to answer such new objections or difficulties, as may be started, to which good answers have not yet been made.

And whereas I have not yet met with a convenient purchase of lands of inheritance for accomplishing such my intention, I do therefore will and ordain (in case it shall please God to take me hence before such settlement be made) that all that my Messuage or dwelling House in St. Michael Crooked Lane, London, which I hold by lease for a certain number of years yet to come, shall stand and be charged, during the remainder of such term as shall be to come and unexpired, at the time of my decease, with the payment of the clear yearly rent and profits that shall from time to time be made thereof (Ground rent, taxes, and necessary reparations being first to be deducted) to be paid to such learned Divine, or preaching minister, for the time being, by quarterly payments; that is to say, at Midsummer, Michaelmass, Christmas, and Lady-Day; the first payment to begin at such of the said feasts as shall first happen next after my decease; and shall be made to such learned Divine, or preaching minister, as shall be in the employment at the time of my death, during his continuance therein; And I will, that after my death, Sir John Rotherham,[115] Sergeant at Law, Sir Henry Ashurst of London, Knight and Baronet, Thomas Tenison,[116] Doctor in Divinity, and John Evelyn,[117] Senior, Esq; and the survivors, or survivor, of them, and such person or persons as the survivor of them shall appoint to succeed in the following Trust, shall have the election and nomination of such Lecturer; and also shall and may continue and appoint him, for any term, not exceeding three years; and at the end of such term, shall make a new election and appointment of the same, or of any other learned minister of the gospel, residing within the City of London, and extent of the Bills of Mortality, at their discretions.

---

[115] **Rotherham, Sir John (1630-1696):** He was the son of Thomas Atwood Rotherham, vicar of Pirton, Hertfordshire, and of Boreham, Essex. He studied at Oxford graduating with a B.A. in 1649, and an M.A. in 1652. In 1653 Rotherham was incorporated at Cambridge. In 1647 he was admitted a member of Gray's Inn, where he was called to the bar in 1655, was elected ancient in 1671, and treasurer in 1685-6. He was knighted in 1688. He was a friend of Robert Boyle, who made him one of the trustees of his lecture. Rotherham died about 1696.

[116] **Tenison, Thomas (1636-1715):** He was archbishop of Canterbury and had been born, according to the parish register, on 29th September 1636 at Cottenham, Cambridgeshire. It was during his ministry in the large parish of St. Martin-in-the-Fields that he came at once into prominence, and during the eleven years he was rector he met almost all of the most eminent men of the day.

[117] **Evelyn, John (1620-1706):** Evelyn was a typical country gentleman of the Restoration period. He was born at Wotton, 31st October 1620. He was on friendly terms with John Wilkins, Bishop of Chester, and with Robert Boyle, to whom he made suggestions that contributed to the establishment of the Royal Society. In 1661 Evelyn was chosen a fellow of the Society and acted as secretary to it in 1672. He later communicated significantly with Bentley, and as one of Boyle's trustees appointed Bentley to the first Boyle lectureship.

Postscript

The following anecdote, relating to Mr. Boyle's father, has been communicated to me since the foregoing pages have been printed off viz. Mr. Budgell, in his life of the late Earl of Orrery, [p.19] observes, that Richard Boyle Esq.; upon his return to Ireland, 1603, began to think of taking a second wife, and accordingly made choice of Catherine, the only daughter of Sir Geoffrey Fenton: but as that match was occasioned by an uncommon accident, which is not mentioned by Mr. Budgell, I shall, according to the best of my remembrance, give you an account of it as I found it in the works of a judicious Divine, who was intimately acquainted with the Countess of Warwick, Daughter of Mr. Boyle, by the Lady we are speaking of. The fact in short is this; One morning, that accomplished gentleman, Richard Boyle, Esq., paid a visit to Sir Geoffrey Fenton, Master of the Rolls, on some affairs of consequence; and Sir Geoffrey being very busy in his closet, looking over some papers, did not come down so soon as usual. But when he came and found that Mr. Boyle had waited for him, he very handsomely asked his pardon, assuring him, that he had known Mr. Boyle waited for him, he would have come down immediately.

Mr. Boyle smiled; and returning the compliment very agreeably, told Sir Geoffrey, that he did not, by any means, think the time long, because he had been diverting himself with his pretty little daughter (who was then in arms, and about two years old) and further added, that he had been courting her with a view of her becoming his wife: Sir Geoffrey, to carry on the pleasantry, told him he would be loath to stay so long for a wife, (being then a young widower) but Mr. Boyle seriously affirmed he would, in case Sir Geoffrey would give his consent; accordingly Sir Geoffrey gave his word he would, and Mr. Boyle gave him fresh assurances of his real design in that respect; and they both fulfilled their promises. The incident of this visit, entirely occasioned by Sir Geoffrey tarrying longer in his apartment than usual, gave rise to a treaty of marriage, which very much contributed to the happiness of Mr. Boyle's life, and the inestimable advantages the latest posterity will reap from the unparalleled munificence of his son, by this lady, the honourable Robert Boyle, Esq.

An epistle
humbly addressed to the Right Hon. John,
Earl of Orrery.
By L. Theobald

Agnosco procerem———Juven.

If grief, or dear respect, have made me slow
To wound your bosom with returns of woe,
While I presume a patron lost to mourn,
And pay due tribute o'er your father's urn;
If, conscious of my weak and falt'ring pow'r,
I wish'd, and waited, that the rolling hour
Some genius, fitter to the task, might raise,
At once, to weep his death, and sing his praise;
Forgive the motives, Sir, that sway'd my breast,
And choak'd passion, labouring, tho' represt.

Forgive me too, if, when I backward trace,
And view with mem'ry's eye his ev'ry grace,
I dare confess those transports they inspir'd;
I lov'd with equal pace, as I admir'd:
Lov'd, yet rever'd. As men on beauty gaze,
But find desire chastis'd by virtue's blaze;
Such awe dwelt round him, it awak'd a fear;
Familiar boldness durst not press too near.
Love and respect their stated limits know,
Respect decreas'd not, as affection grew.

In port majestick, and in aspect clear;
Candid, tho' grave, reserv'd, but not severe,
For condescension, soft'ning decent state,
Proclaim'd the friendly, and preserv'd the great.

With what a charm did he his thoughts dispense!
How temper the resistless force of sense!
Hold wonder chain'd with fresh delight to hear,
And to attention tune the ravish'd ear!
Strong eloquence, convey'd with winning art,
Surpriz'd, yet took possession of the heart:
We doubted, which we felt in most excess,
His strength of reas'ning, or his mild address.
That pleasure is no more: Penurious fate
Lends few great blessings, and contracts their date,
Heav'n's choicest gifts to swift discomfort turn,
We scarce can taste 'em, e'er we're doom'd to mourn,
Your loss, my Lord, the common lot transcends;
All bury fathers, but all lose not friends.
Such sympathy of soul with him you shar'd.
Your thoughts were kindred, as your actions pair'd
Congenial virtues in two bosoms shewn,
Which neither copied, Each might call his own,
Thence comfort dawns, that, tho' of him depriv'd,
I see patron in the son reviv'd.

Permit me, Sir, to turn my eyes on you,
And hope new pleasures rising to my view.
Be, what your father was; and sweetly blend
A double grace, the patron and the friend!
But that's a private wish:—- You must be more;
And shine in all the parts of fame he bore:
The abstract of your race! In whom we find
The statesman, soldier, and the scholar join'd:
Nor thought they, so adorn'd, our humble Bays,
Wreath'd with their laurels, stain'd the warrior's
praise.

O, for a Homer's fire, or Virgil's art,
To breathe the wishes of my ardent heart!
An heart, that glows with such unfeign'd desires
As zeal oft prompts, but flatt'ry ne'er inspires!
When that ignoble motive taints her strain,
Punish the muse, my Lord, with just disdain.

Fir'd with your noble ancestor's renown,
Born to outshine their annals with your own;
Rich in their honours, and enlarg'd of soul,
Come forth and emulate the mighty roll
Come forth, the publick hope, and publick care;
And answ'ring ev'ry wish and ev'ry pray'r.
Firm to the rules which conscious virtue lends;
Firm to your country's rights, and honour's friends:
Scorning to bow you to a court's controul,
With venal voice against the bent of soul.

Thus had I wish'd, with fondness void of art,
And deck'd you up a Boyle in ev'ry part.
As if, perhaps, ambitiously I meant
To share those glories I in fancy lent.
But wishes came too late, and lost their aim;
For you prevent them, and assert your fame.
While tir'd imagination lags behind,
Lab'ring to trace the beauties of your mind.

Virtue! Unenvy'd, but divine estate!
The rare, the best companion of the Great!
The treasure of the wise, that still expands,
And swells beneath the glorious spendthrift's hands!
That, when unwasted, still becomes the less;
When blessing others, does its owner bless.
This wealth, my Lord, you hold in ample store;
An ever-spreading, undiminish'd ore:
A shining mass, so properly your own,

Inherited, it seems deriv'd from none.
If on your private stock you e'er refin'd,
'Twas when to Boyle an Hamilton was join'd:
But if in that some avarice you shewed,
You grew a miser for the Publick Good.

Long may she live, and still, as now, impart
Joy to your eyes, and comfort to your heart!
In such rare union bounteous heav'n is proud
To mark its fav'rites from th' unworthy croud.
Still may that bounteous Heav'n propitious shed
Its choicest influence on your nuptial bed!
And as the cirling years their course maintain,
May each be fruitful, till a blended train
Of beauteous offspring your just smiles divide;
The mother's rapture, and the father's pride!

Nor thou, O Boyle, disdain (when time shall spare,
And yield you vacant from the Patriot's care,)
In soft paternal pleasure to unbend;
The tender father, and instructive friend:
While, pleas'd the blooming heroes round you shine,
Patricians all in virtue, as in line.

FINIS

Appendix I

The Epistles of Phalaris and "The Battle of the Books"

Background to the debate

This debate, largely carried on through the medium of literary pamphlets, was only the latest salvo in a struggle that had begun in the French Academy over 30 years earlier. There were three central planks to the debate

The relative value of ancient and modern scholarship and literature.

The "struggle for control over textual authority at every level including notes marginalia prefaces indexes glossaries appendices and commentaries "scholarly annotation to be a source of contention over the nature of early modern textuality" [Jack Lynch ***Preventing Play: Annotating the Battle of the Books"]***

The interpretation of history and the relationship between "human understanding and knowledge"

Protagonists

William Temple (1628-1699): He was a career diplomatist and for a time Jonathan Swift's employer

Richard Bentley (1662-1742): He was Keeper of the King's Library, a famous critic and philologist.

William Wotton (1555-1727): English scholar, Cambridge Don and Churchman.

Charles Boyle 4th Earl of Orrery (1676-1731)

Jonathan Swift (1667-1745)

Alexander Pope (1688-1744)

Key Events

1690: Sir William Temple publishes *"Essay upon Ancient and Modern Learning"*

1694: William Wotton publishes a reply to Temple, *"Reflections on Ancient and Modern Learning"*

1695: Charles Boyle publishes *"Epistles of Phalaris"*

1697: Richard Bentley publishes *A dissertation upon Phalaris* in a second edition of Wotton's *Reflections*

1699: Boyle publishes *Dr. Bentley's dissertation on the Epistles of Phalaris, and the fables of Aesop, examin'd"*

1699: Bentley publishes *A dissertation upon the epistles of Phalaris., with an answer to the objection of the Honourable Charles Boyle Esq.*

1704: Swift publishes *"A full and true account of the Battel fought last Friday between the ancient and the modern books in St. James's Library"*

1729 Alexander Pope publishes *"Dunciad Variorum"*

Key Issues

One of the key issues in the debate was the relationship between text and analysis. The "Moderns" held that analysis was an essential tool in rendering much of literature accessible. This is most cogently illustrated by the lengths to which Bentley went in his edition of Horace. While published in 1726, Lewis Theobald illustrates this preoccupation even more graphically in his *Shakespeare Restored*. Following "132 pages of minutely documented 'restoration' of Hamlet" he adds an appendix 62 pages long.

Temple's *Essay upon Ancient and Modern Learning* set out to defend the position and quality of the original over the "Moderns" claims that both the analysis itself and its validation or invalidation of the text contextualised and qualified the text. He selected the Epistles of Phalaris and the writings of Aesop as examples of quality on behalf of the "Ancients". The key concern of the "Ancients" was that by such invasion of the text the critic was interfering with the interface between the reader and the writer. It was bestowing on the critic the same rights as those of the writer and thus the same level of significance

Boyle was requested by Temple to produce an edition of the Epistles of Phalaris. The refusal of Bentley to provide Boyle with access to some material in the Library added a further dimension of class bias. Boyle in his criticism of the "Moderns" rounded on Bentley attacking him for ill breading and not showing due deference to his 'betters'.

Bentley and Wotton were able to use their expertise and methods to prove the merit of textual criticism. Bentley illustrated that in both style and chronology Phalaris could not have been written before the birth of Christ and in so doing he invalidated the entire argument of Temple and Boyle.

The debate continued for many years and led to the publication by Swift of the *Battle of the Books* in 1704. Swift was concerned not only to support the cause of the "Ancients" but set out to preserve the integrity of his own writing. He does not directly address the arguments but ridicules and exaggerates the methods of the "Moderns". In his satirical allegory he also settles scores with Dryden and Cowley. The key figures of Bentley and Wotton are defeated by Boyle in the "Battle". The ultimate irony for Swift is that the *Battle of the Books*, while magnificent in its own right, is undoubtedly enhanced by a serious examination of the historical and literary context in which it was produced.

Outcomes

The victors in the debate were quite clearly the "Moderns." Despite the preoccupation of those on the side of the "Ancients" it could be said that only textual analysis and comment made the classics "accessible" to many. While the views of Bentley and Wotton on the origins of the *Epistles of Phalaris* were undoubtedly correct, it was in their approach to scholarly methodology that their legacy is predominant. Despite this, the debate is now best remembered for spawning the two masterpieces of Pope and Swift. Miriam Starkman in her book on the *Tale of a Tub* accurately summarises "Rarely has so great a book been written in a lost cause."

Modern Echoes

This debate has strong and relevant echoes for the modern reader. The situation in modern education and the arts in which creativity and "talent" are currently given hegemony over craft and application is one. Another is the growing anarchic approach to spelling and grammar and indeed the apparent preoccupation in some academic circles with form over content and freshness of approach.

A recent newspaper article (published in the Sunday Times 3 August 2003) illustrates how sensitive even modern writers can be with their books and sources. Apparently Thomas Hardy sourced much of his narratives, particularly the Mayor of Casterbridge, from newspaper articles of the time and was extremely anxious to conceal this. One has to say that this great novel is in no way compromised by the research source.

Appendix II

Contents of the Following Memoirs

Some account of the famous Phalaris. The Sicilian Tyrant
The story of Perillus
Character of Phalaris
The Greeks Aversion to Monarchy
Phalaris's Victories and conquests
His epistles looked upon as genuine for many ages past
Highly admired by the ancients and moderns
Commended by Suidas, Stobaeus, and Photius
Aretine's Encomium upon Phalaris and his Epistles
Sir William Temple's Character of the Epistles of Phalaris
Dr. Bentley of a very different opinion from all these great men
Sir William Temple and the Doctor both right in appealing to the letters themselves
Phalaris's letter to Polistratus and Daiscus
To Axiochus
To Polignotus
To Evensus
To Ariphaetes
To Aristomenes
To Nicias
To Nicaeus
To the Leontines
To Demaratus
To Paurolas
To the same
To Orfilochus
To Stesichorus
To the Children of Stesichorus
To the daughters of Stesichorus
To Philodemus
To Amphinomus
Conclusion of a letter to Agemortus
The Doctor's arguments to prove these Epistles spurious, not conclusive
Mr. Boyle's famous reply to the Doctor's Dissertation
The Doctor writes again, and unfortunately aims at being witty
Mr. Boyle congratulated on all hands upon his victory
Sir Samuel Garth's compliment to him
Some Cambridge wags make an unlucky pun upon the Doctor
The Doctor has his merit
Mr. Boyle suspected of being assisted by a Club of Wits
Vindicated on this head
Character of his comedy, entitled, As you find it

Index

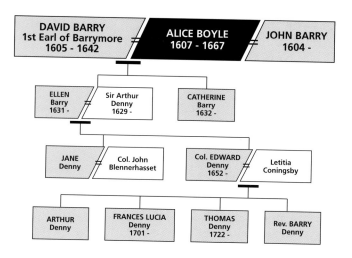

DAVID BARRY
1st Earl of Barrymore
1605 - 1642

ALICE BOYLE
1607 - 1667

JOHN BARRY
1604 -

ELLEN
Barry
1631 -

Sir Arthur
Denny
1629 -

CATHERINE
Barry
1632 -

JANE
Denny

Col. John
Blennerhasset

Col. EDWARD
Denny
1652 -

Letitia
Coningsby

ARTHUR
Denny

FRANCES LUCIA
Denny
1701 -

THOMAS
Denny
1722 -

Rev. BARRY
Denny

Descendants of Dorothy Boyle

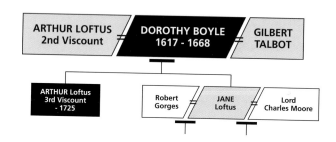

ARTHUR LOFTUS
2nd Viscount

DOROTHY BOYLE
1617 - 1668

GILBERT
TALBOT

ARTHUR Loftus
3rd Viscount
- 1725

Robert
Gorges

JANE
Loftus

Lord
Charles Moore

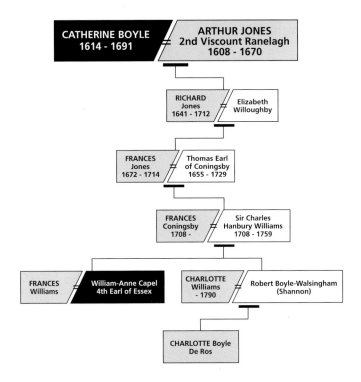

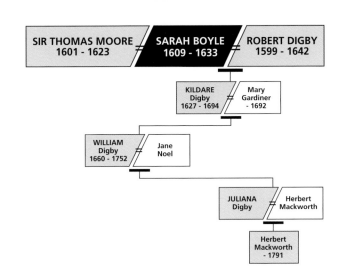

Descendants of Sarah Boyle

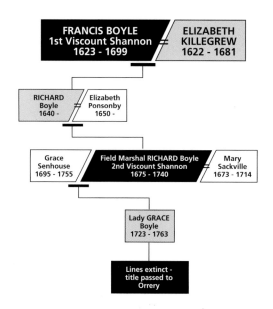

FRANCIS BOYLE
1st Viscount Shannon
1623 - 1699

ELIZABETH KILLEGREW
1622 - 1681

RICHARD Boyle 1640 -

Elizabeth Ponsonby 1650 -

Grace Senhouse 1695 - 1755

Field Marshal RICHARD Boyle
2nd Viscount Shannon
1675 - 1740

Mary Sackville 1673 - 1714

Lady GRACE Boyle 1723 - 1763

Lines extinct - title passed to Orrery

Descendants of Roger Boyle

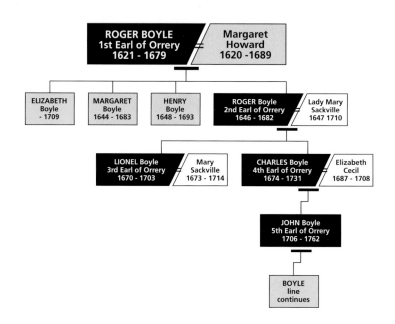

ROGER BOYLE
1st Earl of Orrery
1621 - 1679

Margaret Howard
1620 -1689

ELIZABETH Boyle - 1709

MARGARET Boyle 1644 - 1683

HENRY Boyle 1648 - 1693

ROGER Boyle
2nd Earl of Orrery
1646 - 1682

Lady Mary Sackville 1647 1710

LIONEL Boyle
3rd Earl of Orrery
1670 - 1703

Mary Sackville 1673 - 1714

CHARLES Boyle
4th Earl of Orrery
1674 - 1731

Elizabeth Cecil 1687 - 1708

JOHN Boyle
5th Earl of Orrery
1706 - 1762

BOYLE line continues

Descendants of Joan Boyle

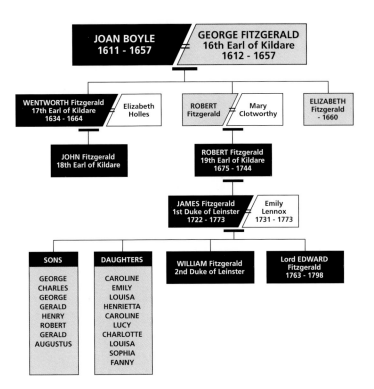

JOAN BOYLE
1611 - 1657

GEORGE FITZGERALD
16th Earl of Kildare
1612 - 1657

WENTWORTH Fitzgerald
17th Earl of Kildare
1634 - 1664

Elizabeth
Holles

ROBERT
Fitzgerald

Mary
Clotworthy

ELIZABETH
Fitzgerald
- 1660

JOHN Fitzgerald
18th Earl of Kildare

ROBERT Fitzgerald
19th Earl of Kildare
1675 - 1744

JAMES Fitzgerald
1st Duke of Leinster
1722 - 1773

Emily
Lennox
1731 - 1773

SONS

GEORGE
CHARLES
GEORGE
GERALD
HENRY
ROBERT
GERALD
AUGUSTUS

DAUGHTERS

CAROLINE
EMILY
LOUISA
HENRIETTA
CAROLINE
LUCY
CHARLOTTE
LOUISA
SOPHIA
FANNY

WILLIAM Fitzgerald
2nd Duke of Leinster

Lord EDWARD
Fitzgerald
1763 - 1798

Descendants of Richard Boyle

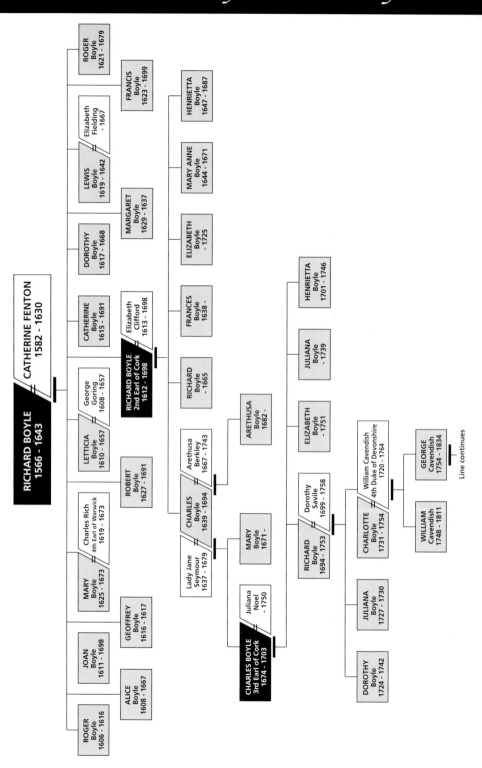